Poetry and its Background

Poetry and its Background

Illustrated by Five Poems
1470-1870

E. M. W. TILLYARD

LITT.D.

Master of Jesus College
Cambridge

BARNES & NOBLE, Inc., New York
Publishers · Booksellers · Since 1873

PUBLISHED BY
Chatto & Windus Ltd
42 WILLIAM IV STREET
LONDON, WC2

*

Clarke, Irwin & Co Ltd
TORONTO

Originally published 1948
under the title of
Five Poems
Retitled 1955
Second Impression 1961

PRINTED BY THE REPLIKA PROCESS
IN GREAT BRITAIN BY
LUND HUMPHRIES
LONDON · BRADFORD

Contents

Illustrations

PREFACE

I HAVE explained the aims of this book in the introductory chapter. I wish here to say a word about the title. The last of the five poems, Swinburne's *Hertha*, was written in 1870. In what year Henryson wrote the *Testament of Cresseid* we do not know. Skeat conjectured 1460; Gregory Smith, who edited Henryson for the Scottish Text Society, dated his working career 1470-1500. Thus 1470 is a possible date for the poem, and for the sake of the title I have used it, to match the 1870 of *Hertha*.

Since this book assumes a knowledge of the poems' texts and the opportunity to refer to them, it is only fair to the reader that I should give what help I can in these matters. The *Ancient Mariner* is so well known and so accessible that no help is necessary. Dryden's *Ode on Anne Killigrew* and Swinburne's *Hertha* are less known and less accessible. For this reason, and since they are comparatively short, I have included them at the end of this volume. Henryson's *Testament of Cresseid* and Sir John Davies's *Orchestra* are too long for such inclusion. I had therefore better say where these two poems can be found. There are convenient separate editions of the *Testament of Cresseid*, one by Bruce Dickins, 1931, the other (with some inaccuracies and faulty punctuation) in the Cambridge Plain Texts, 1926. The poem is included in Hilda M. R. Murray's selections from Henryson (with useful annotations for those who find the early Scottish language difficult), 1930; in the seventh volume (*Chaucerian and Other Pieces*) of Skeat's Chaucer, 1897; and in M. M. Gray's *Scottish Poetry from Barbour to James VI*, 1935. And there are, of course, editions of the whole of Henryson. For Davies's *Orchestra* there is not so wide a choice of editions. The most accessible is my edition of the poem, 1945. The other separate edition, edited by R. S. Lambert in 1922, is limited. *Orchestra* is printed in the *Oxford Book of Six-*

PREFACE

teenth Century Verse but without six of the most beautiful and important stanzas; and in *Some Longer Elizabethan Poems* in Arber's Garner, 1882 and 1905. A. B. Grosart published editions of all Sir John Davies's poems in 1869 and 1876.

To one not familiar with medieval English Henryson's *Testament of Cresseid* may seem formidable. But it is not really a difficult poem, and a little work with glossary and notes should soon make it readable. There are references to it in my sections on the other poems but not so many as to render the whole book unintelligible without the section on Henryson. Anyone genuinely defeated by him can get something out of the book from reading the other sections only. I write thus, because this book (like most of my others) is intended less for the specialist than for the general reader of serious literature.

I wish to record my gratitude to Mrs Olwen Campbell for calling my attention to the importance of Clough's poem in honour of Truth; to the President of Magdalen for suggesting that a Fuseli drawing might provide an analogy with the *Ancient Mariner*; to Prof. Heinrich Straumann of the University of Zurich for procuring me photographs of the two of Fuseli's drawings that seemed to me the most suitable; and to Mr Francis Wormald, of the Department of Manuscripts in the British Museum, for information about the Lydgate manuscript that provided my analogy with *The Testament of Cresseid*. I am indebted to the Trustees of the British Museum and to the Boston Museum of Fine Arts for permission to use photographs of works of art in their possession. The Walpole Society and *Country Life* have each kindly allowed me to use one of their photographs.

E. M. W. T.

INTRODUCTORY

THIS short book is an experimental attempt to present some of the contents of histories of literature in an abbreviated form through particular examples. Histories as against brief outlines of literature, because of the mass of detail they comprise, usually fail to make a vivid impression and turn for practical purposes into books of reference. As such they may be most valuable, but this is not what they set out to be. They purport to give information about separate authors, to deliver critical opinions on them, and to place them in the general thought-background of their epochs. Their method is usually that of the medieval chronicle or chronicle poem, beginning with A and traversing the whole alphabet to Z. So much detail is inimical to any vivid generalisation. It may be that a more selective method will prove more emphatic, at any rate for the beginner. Nor need such a method sacrifice the whole of that continuity which is implied by the very word *history*. If the series A to Z is continuous, it follows that B will in some way imply both A and C. I have thought therefore that as an experiment it might be worth dealing with a few pregnant instances, in the hope that general notions may tell more strongly when reached through the particular and that the changes of temper or doctrine observable from one instance to another may suggest a continuous development. There is warrant for this method in Santayana's *Interpretations of Poetry and Religion*.

I have spent a good deal of thought in choosing my examples. I preferred poems to prose works as being more concentrated and I have chosen poems of manageable length, neither very long nor very short. I hope the reader will agree that the poems are both concentrated and highly typical of their ages. Two happy accidents have blessed the choice. Each poem belongs to a different century with intervals of roughly a hundred years. And, more important, the interconnections are far more numerous than I could have expected between poems chosen each entirely for its own sake in relation to its own age.

There is, it must be admitted, one inevitable defect in the method. However carefully the examples are chosen, they cannot, if drastically limited in number, include all the main marks of the epoch to which they belong. Vividness can be purchased only at the price of partiality.

I must add something on the scope of my comments on the five poems, for in mentioning histories of literature I do not wish to imply that I shall be concerned with all the topics contained in these books.

F. W. Bateson in his *English Poetry and the English Language* has argued that a true history of literature can deal only with literary things, such as diction and prosody; and in theory he may be right. But it remains true that in actual practice we do not appreciate most things we read, from the purely literary side. Our appreciation is mixed; in a way it is not, when we listen to most music. Now though it is fruitless to deplore a mixture of appeals in literature, some mixtures may be better than others, and it is important that we should recognise and foster the best. To my mind the alien, non-literary matters that mix most readily with literature are the prevalent ideas, the current commonplaces, the notions least paraded and most taken for granted, in a word the mythology, of a given epoch. These are things that get into all great literature. But one must distinguish. Some of these ideas are perennial; and it is one of the habits of literary criticism to detect behind the different techniques and the conflicting thought-forms of past epochs the great commonplaces that bind the whole human race together. But some, though widespread and passionately held, are local and temporary, the characteristic commonplaces of this or that country and epoch. And these are proper material for the historians of literature. It is with them that I am chiefly concerned in this book.

2

INTRODUCTORY

But I am far from wishing to consider these topical commonplaces in isolation, for it is precisely the interplay between thought and form that constitutes a main pleasure of reading. Let me illustrate by a well-known passage, Brutus's perplexed soliloquy in *Julius Caesar* before the murder.

> *Between the acting of a dreadful thing*
> *And the first motion all the interim is*
> *Like a phantasma or a hideous dream:*
> *The genius and the mortal instruments*
> *Are then in council; and the state of man*
> *Like to a little kingdom suffers then*
> *The nature of an insurrection.*

Here it is the literary qualities that first tell on us: the rhythm, the choice and collocation of words. Next comes the dramatic context, Brutus in his great perplexity, a situation of permanent human interest. But beyond these and stimulated initially by them there naturally insinuates itself an alien curiosity about the thought, about the cosmic and ethical connotations. There is obviously so much behind the passage. And curiosity will discover there the whole elaborate conception (an Elizabethan commonplace) of the universe as a system of many correspondences: in this passage the microcosm of man corresponding to the state or body politic. And when our curiosity is satisfied, the process is reversed, for with added knowledge we return to the literary qualities of the passage with fresh appetite.

The above example illustrates the process I seek to promote in this book. But I have not always been able to proceed so simply. As a preliminary I have sometimes been compelled to expound difficulties of meaning or to correct what I think misleading interpretations. But, that done, I speak of the literary value of the poems, for it is first (and perhaps only) through that value that the reader naturally desires to know something of the ideas they take for granted or strive to express. For the ideas them-

3

selves, I choose to speak less of the permanent human commonplaces than of those that are the peculiar mark and property of the age. Last, I shall include remarks on how each poem differs from its fellows in certain assumptions it makes about the world order; how it implies a changed or distinct climate of opinion and belief. The final stage in the process, that of applying the knowledge of the poem's setting to a new appreciation of the poem's value, I leave to the reader. The extent to which he does actually succeed in that process will be the exact measure of the success of my experiment.

The book is meant to be simple and unambitious. The actual ideas mentioned are in their very nature elementary. A difficulty here arises. It is easy enough to write of the platitudes of past ages, but to be natural and unembarrassed in writing of those near our own age is hard. I have tried to write of Swinburne in the same tone as of the others, but I have probably failed.

Finally, I have tried hard to let the poems tell their own story rather than to read my preconceived notions into them. Certainly (to give but one instance) before I began reading *Hertha* closely I had not the least notion that it contained the doctrine of Fascism. This came as an utter surprise. I only hope that this instance is the rule and not the exception.

In order to relate each poem more emphatically to its age I have illustrated it by a single example of roughly contemporary art. Perfect analogies between poetic and pictorial are not to be expected, but partial analogies can be very helpful. There are brief notes on the illustrations, at the end of the book.

The Parting of Troilus and Cressida

HENRYSON

The Testament of Cresseid 1470?

I

WE know little about Henryson. Gregory Smith, who edited his works, wrote:

> These are the only facts of Henryson's personal history: first, that he flourished in the latter half of the fifteenth century; secondly, that he was a resident, and probably a native of Dunfermline; and, thirdly, that he was a master of the Grammar School controlled by the Benedictine Abbey of that royal burgh.

But these facts are useful. They tell us that Henryson was an educated man (he may well have been a graduate of St Andrews University, founded early in the fifteenth century). If he was educated, it was in the common lore of western Europe; and his situation on the fringe of the civilised world does not make him less representative of the Middle Ages than if he had been educated at Oxford or Paris or Bologna. So for the purpose of displaying through a particular poem the habits of mind of the late Middle Ages Henryson should do perfectly well. But more people possessed such a qualification than could write memorable poems; and, if the medievalism is to interest us, the poem containing it must first win our affection. I begin then with the literary merit of the *Testament of Cresseid*.

Although Henryson learnt much of his craft from Chaucer and although his poem continues and assumes in the reader a knowledge of Chaucer's *Troilus and Criseyde*, he does not really compete with his master, nor does his poem suffer when compared with its source. In temper the *Testament of Cresseid* is tragic and as such it is nearer akin

to some of the ballads and to the later books of Malory's
Morte Darthur than is the essential comedy of Chaucer.
And through being truly tragic it takes itself right out of
its medieval setting and allies itself to the tragic writings
of all ages. True, when Henryson calls the poem "this
tragedie" he meant no more by "tragedie" than the simple
medieval notion of a human being, of whatever character
and by whatever sequence of events, falling from prosperity into adversity; but in actual fact his poem fulfils
more exacting tragic standards. Cresseid's character is not
subtle or complicated but it is sufficiently mixed to approximate her to the requirements of Aristotle. She is far
from being a saint but she is no villain. Indeed, in herself
she is more good than bad, but her errors of weakness and
vanity co-operated with the turn of events in causing her
ruin. We pity her misfortune and we are afraid because
her own misfortune is the type of what may befall the run
of humanity.

The tragic emotion is swift and concentrated and can
only be conveyed by corresponding poetical means.
Henryson is free from the besetting medieval vice of pro-
lixity and joins the successfully tragic writers of all ages
by the economy and the emphasis with which he tells his
tale. When he is ornate (and he can be so after the fashion
of his age) it is in the pauses of the action.

There still exists so strong a prejudice against the
notion that a medieval poet (apart from Chaucer) could be
an accomplished artist, and the critics have said so little
about the art of the *Testament of Cresseid*, that I will speak
at some length on the economy and emphasis mentioned
above and on other matters of style: first in point of language, secondly in point of construction.

The Scottish form of northern English, Henryson's
native speech, was naturally powerful and emphatic, but
rough; and yet, when skilfully used, it could achieve a
surprising degree of sweetness. Henryson achieves emphasis and holds our attention by his great skill in achiev-
ing linguistic and rhythmic contrasts. A common habit of

rhetoric in the Middle Ages was that of saying the same thing twice in a pattern of balance. It is best known through its survival in the English Prayer Book, it persisted into (for instance) the polite chronicle writing of Hall in the reign of Henry VIII and the prose of Lyly, and it was laughed at in some of the comic writing of Shakespeare. Henryson accepts the convention but puts it to skilful use. He employs it only when he is at leisure and in order to make more emphatic his great power of short intense and moving statements. The poem begins:

> *Ane doolie sessoun to ane cairfull dyte*
> *Suld correspond, and be equivalent.*

The second line is rhetorically redundant. But Henryson here is at leisure; he can afford to be conventionally (and for that age decently) expansive. Similarly in stanza 31, describing the horses of Phoebus, he writes

> *The third Peros, richt hait and richt fervent,*

and again he is at leisure, for it would not do to scant his solemn description of the planetary gods assembled to judge Cresseid. But whenever the action is intense, or even when he merely means business, his language is swift packed and simple. The last line of almost every stanza is of this kind, and these lines give the predominant impression. For emphatic simplicity take the last line of stanza 18,

> *Allace that ever I maid yow sacrifice.*

This *last* line is the *beginning* of Cresseid's blasphemous speech and is in diction and in rhythm the abrupt blurting out of a sheer blasphemy, one of the crises of the poem. Dramatically it simply could not be bettered. Or take the final line of the penultimate stanza, the final words of the inscription in golden letters on the tomb of Cresseid, who

> *Under this stane, lait lipper, lyis deid.*

The line is forceful and plain, to brutality; and that this plainness should have been put in golden letters is anything but accidental. Sometimes Henryson puts redundance and packed sense in close proximity. Take the beginning of stanza 14:

> *This fair Lady in this wyse destitute*
> *Of all comfort and consolatioun,*
> *Richt privelie, but fellowscip, on foot,*
> *Disagysit, passit far out of the toun—*

the first two lines are conventionally rhetorical and redundant: the next seven words recall one of Milton's most concentrated lines:

> *Eyeless in Gaza at the Mill with slaves.*

It is not only by language and rhetoric that Henryson secures variety and contrast; he also manipulates rhythms with masterly skill. There is no better example in English of sound echoing sense than the description of Venus's double-dealing in stanzas 33 and 34. The very first line is illustration enough:

> *Under smyling scho was dissimulait.*

The rhythm of the first two words is bolstered up, suggesting the carefully maintained façade: in the last three words the rhythm collapses and disperses, suggesting both the secretiveness of a whisper and the shifts and eddies behind the façade. Or take the fifth line of stanza 49 describing how men avoid the leper,

> *Quhair thow cummis ilk man sall fle the place.*

The first three words suggest the ponderous and painful motion of Cresseid in her sickness; the rest suggest the speed and hurry of the escaping men. Examples could be multiplied indefinitely, since each fresh reading reveals new subtleties.

Sometimes the rhetorical and rhythmic contrasts are on a larger scale. Conspicuous for ornateness and width of vocabulary, for wealth of alliteration, for strong reverberations of sound are the stanzas describing the planets and their judgement. They are followed by the contrasted

8

simplicity and realism of the child coming to call Cresseid to supper. But when a little lower down Cresseid utters her complaint we compare its ornateness with that of the planet-description, but we contrast the wonderfully dulcet tone, its slow and rich and sinuous stanza form, with the grating violence and abrupt cadences of the description of Saturn, her chief enemy, who had robbed her of the gay life she so exquisitely recalls.

The above larger comparisons and contrasts are matters of structure as well as of style. They lead on to other structural details.

The use of irony seems peculiarly appropriate in tragedy: probably because of its astringent effect and of the concentration given by astringency. Irony rests on a contrast between knowledge and ignorance and is usually consummated by the ignorant person's enlightenment. Oedipus cursing the man responsible for the city's plague does not know that he is the man, but the audience does. Later he learns, and his new enlightenment recalls his old ignorance: different parts of the play are drawn together. Added to such specific cases of knowledge and ignorance there can be the general impression that fate knows so much more about the whole business than the people who actually transact it. Both kinds of irony occur in the *Testament of Cresseid* and they help to bind the parts of the poem together. The most effective example depends on our recollection of Chaucer's poem. There, one of the most brilliant scenes is of Troilus riding down the street and Cresseid watching him: then, she was in her glory and he her *conscious* slave. When, in Henryson's poem, Troilus rides past a second time, she is a leper and he does not even recognise her. Behind the two episodes is the impression of fate's superior knowledge: when Cresseid was proud and watched Troilus securely, fate was already preparing a contrasting episode. In stanza 72 there is irony that Cresseid, in her extreme sickness and unrecognised by Troilus, should yet arouse to such excess the love symptoms in him. Fate as it were staged this extreme instance of his fidelity to prove to Cresseid how precious a thing she had rejected. A beautiful minor example of irony is in the message the child brings to summon Cresseid to supper, after her doom (stanza 52, 7):

The Goddis wait all your intent full weill.

Chalchas meant that Cresseid must have said all the needful prayers by this time. He does not realise that his words can mean with terrible appropriateness that the gods heeded —and punished—the impious tenour of her prayers only too thoroughly. When

He luikit on hir uglie lipper face,

we may take it he was enlightened.

How greatly Henryson minded about knitting his poem tightly can be seen in a single instance of a repeated theme: that of the relations of Esperus, or the evening star Venus, and Saturn. At the beginning the author goes to the window to do homage to the star but he is driven away by the frost, which is the quality of Saturn. In stanza 7 Esperus gives Troilus hope when he has fallen into despair. In stanza 20 Cresseid complains that the seed of love sown in her face has been frozen, and later it is Saturn, the frosty god, who is foremost in punishing her. In stanza 46 Cresseid is described, like the amorous Cleopatra in Shakespeare, as being all air and fire. But now the saturnine chill induces leprosy, which is white like snow though spotted with black. Finally in stanza 58 in the evening after she has entered the lazar-house, the sky is clouded. In other words Esperus cannot be seen, and we are taken back by contrast to the opening of the poem.

The *Testament of Cresseid* is, among other things, a tragedy in the medieval sense, the fall from prosperity to misfortune; and Henryson, though dealing principally with the latter, cannot omit the former. His means are simple and brilliantly effective. Into Cresseid's complaint he inserts two stanzas (60 and 61) in which she recalls her old life at court.

> *Quhair is thy chalmer wantounlie besene*
> *With burely bed and bankowris browderit bene,*
> *Spycis and wyne to thy collatioun,*
> *The cowpis all of gold and silver schene,*
> *The sweit meitis servit in plaittis clene*
> *With saipheron sals of ane gud sessoun,*
> *Thy gay garmentis with mony gudely goun,*
> *Thy plesand lawn pinnit with goldin prene?*
> *All is areir, thy greit royall renoun.*
>
> *Quhair is thy garding with thir greissis gay*
> *And fresche flowris, quhilk the quene Floray*
> *Had paintit plesandly in everie pane,*
> *Quhair thou was wont full merilye in May*
> *To walk and tak the dew be it was day*
> *And heir the merle and mavis mony ane,*
> *With ladyis fair in carrolling to gane,*
> *And se the royal rinks in thair array*
> *In garmentis gay garnischit on everie grane?*

Here the brilliant colours suggest contemporary illumination; and the powerful beat of the verse, the rich alliteration, and the reiterated pressure of the rhyme render with superb success spring and youth at their height when sap and blood flow with the most insistence and jubilation. The stanzas do their work of recollection with great economy and simultaneously set up an emphatic contrast to the loathsomeness of the lazar-house.

Finally, the whole poem is disposed on a firm simple and satisfying plan. There are three clearly articulated crises, each conveyed with strict economy but each relieved by passages of lyrical ornateness. The first is Cresseid's blaspheming the gods (stanzas 18 ff.). This is followed by the elaborate description of the planets. The second is her entry into the lazar-house, the climax of her punishment, and it is followed by her elaborate lyrical complaint. The third is Troilus's passing and alms-giving, by which Cresseid realises the truth and what she has lost. And this is followed by the poem's true resolution: her self-accusation with its lyrical refrain,

> *O fals Cresseid and trew knicht Troylus,*

and her testament. Her death is no crisis but the fitting conclusion.

II

The qualities I have mentioned so far are not specifically medieval; they apply to all poetry. And they unite to make the *Testament of Cresseid* a very fine poem. Further, they should prompt the reader to be curious about other qualities of the poem, which *are* medieval. These are important, first for being essential to the full understanding of the poem and secondly for their historical and moral interest. They are strange qualities we do not share; yet they are interesting because we must have that in our minds which makes them understandable. We, like the medieval people, and they like us, are human beings; and, given the conditions, our minds could work like theirs. Perhaps, in actual fact, they *do* work more in the medieval way than we care to admit.

(a)

THE MORAL SETTING

By far the most important of the medieval presuppositions governing the poem is the theological; and all the more because it is not stated at all but quietly taken for granted. Further, it has been passed over, or, if recognised, misunderstood. People often contrast the kindliness and humanity of Chaucer in *Troilus and Criseyde* with Henryson's harshness and legality in the *Testament of Cresseid*. Henryson, they say, was the true Scots puritan, who anticipated the harshness of John Knox and his fellow-Calvinists towards the sin of sensuality. He was not content to leave things in the air in the tolerant way Chaucer did; he must have rigid justice, an eye for an eye. They are wrong and misunderstand Chaucer's motive in allowing Criseyde to fade out of the poem. Chaucer is first concerned with the feelings of Troilus, and his Criseyde must subserve them. Any elaborate punishment awarded her would upset his scheme. Further, when it suits him, Chaucer can be quite as moral as Henryson; and pre-eminently when he pictures the soul of Troilus looking down from the heavens onto the business of mortals and seeing how trivial it is compared with the eternal verities. On the other hand Henryson is as kind to his Cresseid as he was free to be within the scheme of orthodox theology.

It remains to point out how full and how precise and how centrally medieval is the morality of the *Testament of Cresseid*.

Like Malory and other medieval writers Henryson acknowledges two moral codes: the code of Love and the code of the Church. These codes both conflicted and co-operated. Being founded on an exaltation of sex and on adulterous love, the code of Love conflicted with the Church. But provided the conflict was admitted, provided the practice was allowed to be sinful, the Church was not intolerant. Its disposition was close to that of the modern Catholicism exemplified by Claudel in the *Satin Slipper*. This play takes its title from one of its incidents. The heroine, who is married, is on a journey which she knows will end in adultery. She comes to a wayside image of the Virgin, and, taking off one of her exquisite satin slippers, places it on the Virgin's arm, in token that if she is journeying to sin at least it must be with a halting gait. Even if she does actually sin, she admits she is sinning; and that makes all the difference to her chances of ultimate salvation. To return to the code of Love, once the initial irregularity was granted, the moral rules of service and fidelity were very exacting. And this exactingness was there from the very beginning, being found in the pagan book to which the code of courtly love owed so much, the *Ars Amatoria* of Ovid. This poem, however un-Victorian in temper, has its own morality. At the very beginning Ovid makes it plain that the life of illicit love is hard, that it has its own discipline, and that a vast amount of trouble has to be taken for comparatively insignificant results. The medieval courtly code saw to it that these things were indeed so. It might take several years' probation for the lover to get a kiss, while achievement was comparatively rare. The great principle of the code was the lover's absolute fidelity, which implied a high standard of self-discipline. Indeed, the devotion of the lover to his lady resembled the devotion of the faithful to Mother Church. Hence the code of Love could in its way co-operate with the code of the Church, even preparing its devotees for a transfer of allegiance. This is the doctrine found in Malory's *Morte Darthur*; and it is put with special force in the last chapter of book eighteen, the lyrical passage on May leading to the Queen's Maying in the next book. May is the lover's month,

> for like as herbs and trees bring forth fruit and flourish in May, in like wise every lusty heart that is in any manner a lover springeth and flourisheth in lusty deeds. For it giveth unto all lovers courage, that lusty month of May, in something to constrain him to some manner of thing more in that month than in any other month.

And after enlarging on this theme Malory ends:

> Therefore all ye that be lovers call unto your remembrance the month of May, like as did Queen Guenever, for whom I make here a little mention, that while she lived she was a true lover, and therefore she had a good end.

The second *therefore* in this passage is very important. Guenever's love was adulterous, in accord with the courtly and in conflict with the Church code. But within the courtly code she was a true lover, fulfilling the main condition of absolute fidelity. *Therefore* she was allowed to end her life in the sanctity of a house of nuns.

The two codes operate in the *Testament of Cresseid* precisely as they do in *Morte Darthur*, but the Church code is less evident on account of the pagan setting. This setting may prove confusing to a modern reader because the pagan gods here have mixed functions; so I had better explain it before dealing with the poem's general morality. The chief god is Cupid, and his first and obvious function is that of the traditional ruler of the order of lovers. In the most authoritative work of literature concerned with courtly love, the *Roman de la Rose*, Cupid, the god of love, rules in the allegorical garden:

> *A li se tint de l'autre part*
> *Li Diex d'Amors, cil qui départ*
> *Amoretes à sa devise.*
> *C'est cil qui les amans justise*
> *Et qui abat l'orguel des gens*
> *Et si fait des signors sergens*
> *Et des dames refait bajesses*
> *Quant il les trove trop engresses.*

(Lines 869-76)

In the Chaucerian translation the lines run,

> *And next hir wente on hir other syde*
> *The god of Love, that can devyde*
> *Love, as him lyketh it be.*
> *But he can cherles daunten, he,*
> *And maken folkes pryde fallen*
> *And he can wel these lordes thrallen*
> *And ladies putte at lowe degree*
> *Whan he may hem to proude see.*

But Henryson's Cupid is more than the ruler of the garden of the rose, he is a superior pagan god who convenes a court of other pagan gods, who are also the planets. He is in fact the Eros of Hesiod Plato and Aristotle, oldest of the gods, the creator of order out of chaos, and hence in

15

authority over the others. These other gods are a blend (and an original blend [1]) of pagan mythological deities with planetary rulers. Normally, in medieval writing, the pagan gods kept their mythological attributes, merely giving their names to the planets. Henryson approximates them to the beliefs and fashions of his age by making them mainly astrological. He invests them as deities with the powers usually given to the planets as such. In other words his pagan gods are both ornamental in the conventional medieval way and operative in the way the medieval people really believed the planets to work. Now Cupid as creator and the planets with their influence are separate from their other selves as just described and are parts of the general scheme of God's universe. In stanza 42 Cupid says to them

> *And sen ye ar all sevin deificait,*
> *Participant of devyne sapience,*

and to Henryson's audience divine sapience or wisdom could only bear a solemn theological meaning. Cupid then and the pagan gods in their planetary function belong to the theological code and when Cresseid offends against them she offends against God's holy laws.

We can now deal with the poem's morality and the nature of Cresseid's offence. First, by her infidelity to Troilus she offended against the code of love and against Cupid in his function of dictator of all lovers. And having thus offended, where Guenever was blameless, her chances of virtue under the other code were much less. That is the position when the poem begins. Further, the temple which Calchas served was a place of general worship, where the "pepill far and neir" used to come: in fact the poetical equivalent of a Christian church. And when Cresseid utters her blasphemies there, she does so in an appropriate way, committing two of the deadly sins. First, pride, in that she blames God for her misfortune instead of herself,

---

[1] See M. W. Stearns, *The Planet Portraits of Robert Henryson*, in *Publications of the Modern Languages Association*, 1944, pp. 911-27.

and second, anger, for "angerly scho cryit out". And the
rest of the poem describes the consequences of these sins.
The consequences are not the mere facts that Cresseid
was punished and died a leper but that through the working of God's will she was punished, brought to penitence,
and ended by taking the blame on herself: in fact the story
of her salvation according to the Christian scheme. The
process is beautifully contrived. Early in the poem (stanza
17) for all her subsequent arrogance in blaming the gods
she was inwardly ashamed and could not face the people
in the temple. After this blasphemy she suffers condign
punishment. Her sin was pride, and the infliction of
leprosy ruined the lovely complexion and the courtly
carolling which had been the source of her vanity. However, by itself the leprosy is not enough to make her
repent. In stanza 51, although she regrets her blasphemy
as an act of rashness that has brought trouble on herself,
she does not repent of it but calls the gods "craibit" or
unfairly harsh. And when she enters the lazar-house, her
state of mind is self-pity: she contrasts her present misery
with her past glamour. Then comes the episode of Troilus
riding by and of his great generosity; and with the uprush
of feeling caused by her recognising his worth and what
she had voluntarily rejected, her barrier of pride is quite
broken down and she exclaims,

> *O fals Cresseid and trew knicht Troylus.*

And, most important of all (stanza 80), she blames herself
and no one else,

> *Nane but myself, as now, I will accuse.*

This is the resolution of the poem: the true repentance of
Cresseid and the salvation of her soul. In her testament she
makes what amends she can. Weaned from the lusts of the
flesh she bequeaths her body to be devoured by worms
and toads. In sincere pity and unselfishness she bequeaths
the gold Troilus gave her to the lepers. She returns Troilus
his ring. She dedicates her spirit to Diana, the goddess of

chastity: in other words she aspires, as far as she can, to the monastic life. But the thought that Diomede, who forsook her, still has the brooch and belt which Troilus, who was true, gave her and that she cannot restore them is too cruel and she dies.

Guenever in *Morte Darthur* died a holy nun. Her soul went perhaps to Paradise, perhaps to one of the higher regions of Purgatory. Cresseid's aspiration to be a nun was cut off by death. But she had repented and she could not have been damned. Her soul must have gone to Purgatory, yet with much penance to perform. If Henryson had been austere and a Calvinist he would have counted Cresseid's sin as too rank for forgiveness and committed her soul to Hell. Henryson was not hostile to Cresseid, as he tells us in stanza 13, but he does his best for her according to the laws of his religion.

> *Yit nevertheles quhat ever men deme or say*
> *In scornefull langage of thy brukkilnes,*
> *I sall excuse als far furth as I may*
> *Thy womanheid, thy wisdom and fairnes,*
> *The quhilk Fortoun hes put to sic distres*
> *As hir pleisit, and nathing throw the gilt*
> *Of the, throw wickit langage to be spilt.*

In other words Cresseid's fickleness has been treated too harshly. In extenuation one must remember that she had her good qualities and that fortune was cruel in separating her from Troilus and bringing Diomede in her way. And Henryson goes on to tell how, after all, she was saved.

In this section I set out to speak of religious and ethical matters common to the whole age and exemplified in the *Testament of Cresseid*, matters in themselves unconnected with literature. But they turned out to have a literary bearing. Through them a second plot, that of Cresseid's inward purification, was revealed. The first plot was of her outward punishment and death. As we now read the poem we should bear both plots simultaneously in mind, to the great enrichment of the total significance.

(*b*)

THE STARS

I have spoken above of the use Henryson made of
Esperus or the planet Venus in constructing his poem
and of the poetic majesty of his planet-description. Now
good construction and majestic verse are things easily perceived by a modern, and they can be found in the literature of all periods. Yet the influence of the stars meant so
much more to Henryson and his contemporaries than to
us that we cannot gauge the full effect he produced from
it unless we extend our knowledge. We recognise and
admire how the story is braced by the repeated references
to Esperus, we are pleased and thrilled by the crowded
detail and the high colours by means of which Henryson
renders his pageant of the seven planets. All this Henryson's contemporaries would have felt much as we do, but
their feelings would have been enlarged first by an authentic belief in the power of the stars and by an interest in
the ways that power worked, and secondly by the accident
that in the epoch of Chaucer and his successors this interest
in the stars, always present in the Middle Ages, was
especially fashionable.

It is a modern commonplace that astrology and not
astronomy was current in the Middle Ages and that men
calculated nativities and chose lucky conjunctions of the
stars for important actions. So far the commonplace is
correct; it is the accompanying assumption that such acts
were merely superstitious that is false. There was much
superstition and there were many illicit magical practices
current, but astrology did not belong here. On the contrary the stars were the instruments of God, and to study
them was to study the workings of his will. Henryson's
declaration that his planetary deities partook of divine
wisdom I found useful above as evidence to put before a
modern reader that the planets were more than blind

powers; to a contemporary it would merely be a re-assuring iteration of the obvious and the accepted. Nothing he said about the stars could have given the least offence to the Benedictine Abbey to which his school was attached.

Far from keeping God and the orthodox scheme of salvation in one department and the irrational workings of the stars in another, the Middle Ages looked on the stars as an organic part of God's creation and as the perpetual instruments and diffusers of his will. And like that will they were unsearchable. The following passage from one of the medieval encyclopedists has the true medieval tone:

> Above Saturn, which is the last plainest and highest from us of all the seven planets, is the heaven that men see so full of stars as it were sown, when it is clear time and weather. This heaven that is so starred is the firmament which moveth and goeth round. Of which moving is so great joy, so great melody and so sweet, that there is no man that, if he might hear it, the never after should have talent ne will to do thing that were contrary unto our Lord in anything that might be; so much should he desire to come thither where he might alway hear so sweet melody and be alway with them. Whereof some were sometime that said that little young children heard this melody when they laughed in their sleep; for it is said that then they hear the angels of Our Lord in heaven sing, whereof they have such joy in their sleep. But hereof knoweth no man the truth save God that knoweth all, which setted the stars on the heaven and made them to have such power. For there is nothing within the earth ne within the sea, how diverse it be, but it is on the heaven figured and compassed by the stars; of which none knoweth the number save God only, which at his pleasure numbreth them and knoweth the name of every each of them, as he that all knoweth and all created by good reason.[1]

It was however the planets which had the greatest im-

---

[1] Caxton's *Mirrour of the World*, ed. O. H. Prior. London, 1913, p. 128.

mediate power over human affairs and about whose be-
haviour men could learn most:

> These seven planets been such that they have power on things
> that grow on the earth and abound their virtues more than all the
> other that been on the firmament and more apparently work, like
> as the ancient sage philosophers have ensearched by their wits.[1]

We are apt to underestimate the reasonableness with
which the theory of planetary influences presented itself
to the minds of Chaucer's or Henryson's contemporaries.
For instance, the different seasons of the year obviously
depended on the varying relations of one of the planets,
the sun, to the earth. But though these relations varied
they did so constantly. Hence though the climate of
January differed from that of May, you would expect all
Januaries to be alike. Obviously they were not, and as
obviously because the other planets exerted their diversi-
fying influence. What could be more reasonable?

When Henryson used the planets as the instruments of
Cresseid's punishment he not only implied that her punishment was by God's will but he used the agents which
in contemporary idea were most concerned with human
affairs. He was being as natural as a modern novelist
would be in explaining the adult acts of his characters
through some event of their early years. Further, the conviction that the stars really did work like that would add
terror to what without it is already terrific enough. What
must have been especially terrifying in Henryson was the
concurrence of all the planets. In the normal operation the
influence of one planet balanced or impeded that of another. By a singular concurrence they all combine to
punish Cresseid.

Henryson's astrological knowledge was correct as far as
it went. He gives the planets their proper order; he knows
their different attributes; and when it is Saturn and no
other planet that strikes Cresseid with leprosy he shows
that he understands their different functions. Saturn, with

[1] *Ib.* p. 126.

his frosty nature, pale leaden hue, and livid lips was the planet to which the pale disease of leprosy with its black spots was assigned: an assignment valid into the seventeenth century when Lilly, the astrologer, says that Saturn in Leo causes leprosy.

Such accuracy was important because of the fashionable interest in the details of astrology prevalent in Chaucer's day and inherited by his poetical followers. W. C. Curry in his *Chaucer and the Medieval Sciences* has an interesting chapter on the *Knight's Tale*, in which he expounds the full astrological complexity of that story. Behind the human action (and for contemporary readers making this action more vivid and close to them) is the conflict between the two planets, Saturn and Mars, Saturn defending the interests of his daughter Venus. Arcite has Mars for his protector and the champions he assembles for the tournament are martial in character. Palamon has Venus (and hence Saturn) for his protector and his champions are most carefully and correctly delineated as of saturnine disposition. Arcite wins the actual battle, but Saturn contrives his death by sickness. And in the end Palamon, faithful to Venus, marries his Emily. Curry quite rightly sees that for all its complexity and its topical attraction the machinery of the stars is subsidiary in Chaucer to his interest in his story and in the passions of his characters, but

> in order that this action and these emotions may be rationalised for his readers of the Middle Ages, he has made of scientific astrology a handmaiden to his literary art.

The same is true of Henryson. The *Testament of Cresseid* is first of all a human tragedy but the mechanism of the planets was the natural one for Henryson to use. Through this once living and topical, but now outmoded, complex of belief he can present the eternal human drama more freshly than through other means which though in themselves more reasonable would lack the essential stamp of contemporary vogue.

22

(c)

LOVE OF LIFE AND CONTEMPT
OF THE WORLD

The simple contrast between blossoming and decay, fire and ashes, the bright hair and the skeleton's bone, exists in every age; and I did not mean the earlier mentioned contrast between Cresseid's life at court and her life in the lazar-house to go beyond the perennial commonplace. But in the Middle Ages the contrast took a peculiar form and became rather a conflict. Whereas the Greeks had merely noted and lamented the contrast, with their minds quite easy that blossoming was better than decay, the Middle Ages distrusted the blossoming and the brilliance and thought that decay might really be better as bringing men to perceive a higher blossoming than this world provided. When life was very insecure, such a habit of mind could easily prevail. But with the growth of security, as strong kingdoms arose and orderly towns encircled themselves with walls, and with the revival of art and learning in the twelfth century, men could not help thinking that the present life was very good indeed. The Church, convinced that compared with another life the present life was evil, opposed that thought. It was the special characteristic of the Middle Ages that the two ways of thinking co-existed in a well-developed form; and not merely in opposed groups of people but within the single mind. The worldling who becomes the achieved ascetic, the type of St Augustine and St Francis, is familiar enough, but he belongs to all ages and though frequent in the Middle Ages was not its special mark. Or take an ascetic modern writer, who does not exclude the charms of the senses, T. S. Eliot. In *Ash Wednesday* the vision seen through the window on the stairs is one of sensual pleasure:

At the first turning of the third stair
Was a slotted window bellied like the fig's fruit
And beyond the hawthorn blossom and a pasture scene
A broadbacked figure drest in blue and green
Enchanted the maytime with an antique flute.

But the *balance* is on the side of asceticism; the spiritual journey up the stairs is not prevented by the view. In some men of the Middle Ages love of life and contempt of the world suffered a different adjustment: not a balance but a state of tension in which both opinions existed in an extreme form and neither predominated. The classic exposition of this tension is Petrarch's prose dialogue, the *Secretum*, between the writer and St Augustine. Both opinions are put forward, but the conflict is indecisive; and we are left with them both in their full potency. Chaucer resembles Petrarch in more than one place. *Troilus and Criseyde* shows as strong a relish for living as any poem, but it is entirely sincere in the final scene of the soul of Troilus looking down on the earth and despising the petty affairs that go on in it. The retraction at the end of the *Canterbury Tales* co-exists with rather than cancels the *Merchant's Tale* or the *Wife of Bath's Prologue*.

Now Henryson (to judge by his work as a whole and especially the *Fables*) seems naturally to have been a healthy and kindly person. Unlike Dunbar, whose nature was more violent, he could accept the medieval paradox and endure the tension without much trouble. Yet that paradox is there, in the *Testament of Cresseid*, in brilliant outline. It comes out in the opening description, so close to life and indicating so sensitive a love for it, of the author mending the fire, taking a drink, and settling to read; in the brilliant colour of Jupiter as described among the planets,

As goldin wyre sa glitterand was his hair,
His garmound and his gyis full gay of grene
With golden listis gilt on everie gair,

contrasted with the unflinching application of an other-

worldly morality and with a touch like Cresseid's be-
queathing

> *my corps and carioun*
> *With wormis and with taidis to be rent.*

This dwelling on the corpse and corruption is only a
touch in Henryson's poem yet it allies him to a large
medieval tradition and one which continued beyond the
Middle Ages proper into Elizabethan drama and Donne.[1]
Behind Henryson's touch is the most famous and the most
influential of all the works that dwelt on decay with the
objects of alienating men from the glamour of this life
and of stirring their appetites for a better one, the *De
Contemptu Mundi* of Pope Innocent III. Here is a short
passage in the translation which the Elizabethan, George
Gascoigne, made under the title of the *Drum of Doomsday*:

Let man then, with tears, consider whereof he is made, what he
doth, and what he meaneth to do. Surely he shall find that he
was formed and fashioned of the earth, conceived in sin, born
unto misery, and that he doth lewd things which are not lawful,
filthy things which are not comely, and vain things which are
not expedient. He shall be made fuel for fire, meat for worms,
and matter for corruption. But let me expound these words
more plainly. I should better have said: man is formed and made
of dust clay ashes and a matter much viler which for modesty I
do not name, conceived in the concupiscence of the flesh, in
the fervent heat of lust, in the loathsome stink of desire, and
(that worse is) in the blot and blemish of sin ; born unto pain
sorrow and fear, yea (and that which is most miserable) unto
death. He doth lewd things whereby he offendeth God his
neighbour and himself. He doth filthy facts, whereby he de-
fileth his good name his conscience and his person; and he doth
vain things whereby he neglecteth serious profitable and necessary things. He shall become the fuel for fire which always
burneth and cannot be quenched, the food of worms which
ever gnaw and feed upon him, and the continual mass of corruption which always stinketh and is filthy odious and horrible.

[1] See Theodore Spencer, *Death and Elizabethan Tragedy*, Cambridge,
Mass., 1936.

25

Henryson has none of Innocent's savage hatred of the flesh: nevertheless he does arouse the whole medieval context through his reference to worms and toads and corpses.

But Henryson expresses the medieval paradox most aptly and most beautifully in Cresseid's lament, which is a repertory of medieval commonplaces. The delight in life is obvious, in the gaiety and sensuous beauty of the court. There is no more dazzling description in literature than that in the stanzas already quoted of Cresseid walking in her garden in May, to take the dew and hear the birds sing, then going with the other ladies singing, and seeing "the royal rinks in thair array". But even these two stanzas (60 and 61), quite apart from the later stanzas in the lament describing the leper's life, imply the transience and vanity of all this brilliance. They both begin with the words "Quhair is . . .", and these at once set the stanzas in a large and familiar medieval context. Again and again, and in whatever language—*ubi sunt* or *où sont?*—the medieval writers asked that question; and the answer, whether stated or implied, always was that these things are vanity and that they have passed away. The theme was set in the great Latin poem *De Contemptu Mundi* by Bernard of Morlaix (from which *Jerusalem the Golden* and other English hymns are taken and whose rich texture is the best literary parallel to the earliest stained glass in Chartres Cathedral):

> *Nunc ubi curia pompaque Julia? Caesar, obisti.*

The medieval students in their song *Gaudeamus igitur* began one verse with

> *Ubi sunt qui ante nos*
> *In mundo fuere?*

And the answer to *ubi sunt?* in the last line of the verse is *fuere*: they are dead. Villon ended a ballade with

> *Mais ou est le preux Charlemagne?*

and in another, asking where are various ladies of re-
nowned beauty, he ends each stanza with

Mais ou sont les neiges d'antan?

In beginning his stanzas with *Where is?* Henryson would
summon up instantly the context of decay and mortality
into which Cresseid's once brilliant life is to be set.

Another large context would be suggested when in
stanza 64 Cresseid tells people to use her as a *mirror*: and
a very moral context too. Medieval mirrors were always
didactic, sometimes of what you should imitate, usually of
what you should avoid. And like the paradox of love of life
and contempt of the world they lasted into Elizabethan
days. Hamlet was the glass of fashion, which means that
other people ought to imitate him.

These references to medieval commonplaces are a
source of strength. They attach the *Testament of Cresseid*
instantly to a great tradition; they assure us that Henryson
spoke the language of all western Europe. Through the
repose bred of that assurance Henryson can give us what
is unique, what he alone of men is able to give.

(d)

FIXITY AND REPOSE

Henryson lived in a turbulent age, when the Wars of
the Roses were being fought in England and when his own
country was in a state of political unrest. Further, Scotland
was still backward compared with the rest of western
Europe and still largely barbarous in spite of the un-
doubted if late advent of medieval civilisation. The whole
age, as Huizinga has pointed out with such charm, was
one of fierce extremes and great unrest. Yet the *Testament
of Cresseid*, somewhat impalpably it is true, conveys the
feeling of fixity and repose. However broken and futile
actual life was, however far attainments fell short of aims,
there was agreement on certain great matters of principle.

The Reformation was not far off, but Henryson still belongs to an age of assured and static belief, and that assurance makes itself felt in his poem.

Although he crowds so much into a small space, he is no more in a hurry than is Lydgate with his vast prolixities. His verse, though full of feeling, has yet the coolness of perfectly sound nerves. It is *deliberate* in every sense. When in formal and steady words he begins by saying that a sad tale should accompany foul weather, he goes far beyond a mere *ad hoc* propriety. Such propriety is backed by the assurance that the whole scheme of God's universe was constructed on similar correspondences. Any failure to achieve such propriety was not, as it now would be, a mere error of taste but an offence against the whole nature of the universe. When in one of the wars in the late Middle Ages the envoys of the two sides met in a pavilion to discuss a possible peace, it was noticed that the tapestry on the walls displayed scenes of war. The negotiations were held up till appropriate decoration could be found. Such an act sprang from just those assumptions which peep out in the *Testament of Cresseid*.

The whole tone of the planet-description is that of utter assurance. That one of those planets would in a few years turn out to be a fixed star would have been to Henryson a thought as incredible as it was blasphemous. Behind the description lies a vast weight of authority: treatises on astronomy, ancient, Arabic, and European; summaries in one encyclopedia after another: and all following the same broad lines, however much difference there might be over inessentials. Here was a world, in a way corrupt through the sin of Adam, but yet the visible work of the Creator, immutable in its main design and animated through every particle of its composition: a world in which every part needed every other part and in constant significant motion through the abiding pressure of the providence of God. This was the great fact that more than made up for the appalling turmoils to which in obvious actuality mankind was subjected.

In the social order, too, there was still stability. The estates of the commonwealth were still clearly defined: there was as yet no commercialism in Scotland to create new social orders; there was nothing comparable to the Wars of the Roses in killing off the old aristocracy. All this lies behind the coolness of the lines—cool because the notion that the sentiment could be questioned was infinitely remote—describing Cresseid's reception into the lazar-house (stanza 57):

> *Yit thay presumit for hir hie regrait*
> *And still murning scho was of nobill kin,*
> *With better will thairfoir they tuik hir in.*

The age of Henryson had its full share of difficulties, yet in the above matters it had its advantages. You knew where you were in the biggest matters; you had time to take stock and think; and the pains of a major reorientation were for the time unknown.

SIR JOHN DAVIES

Orchestra 1594

I

I HAVE chosen *Orchestra* principally because it is so typical an Elizabethan poem and because it includes so much. But two superficial resemblances to the *Testament of Cresseid* give the choice a welcome minor aptitude. First, the God of Love presides in both poems; secondly, they are both cast in the form of glosses on greater works. The *Testament of Cresseid* purports to end Chaucer's poem, *Orchestra* to make good an episode missing from the middle of the *Odyssey*.

We know much more of Davies's life than of Henryson's; and what we know gives us the same reassurance: that he was well placed to understand the disposition and the opinions of his age. He was well educated, studied law at the Middle Temple, had his wild and his serious side, and became an important man of affairs. *Orchestra* was written by the time he was twenty-five and it belongs to the very height of Elizabethan as against Jacobean creation: to the age of *Venus and Adonis*, *Love's Labour's Lost*, *Richard III*, the last books of the *Fairy Queen*, the first books of *Laws of Ecclesiastical Polity*, to the end of the period of the University Wits.

If the *Testament of Cresseid* first strikes us as a tragic story, *Orchestra* first captivates us by the compulsion and variety of its music and by the fantasy of its imagination. And readers have been too apt to go no further than this first impression. The learning, the academicism even, and the orderly disposition, evident to careful reading, are as true qualities as the first mentioned. Above all it is the fusion of extravagant expression with academic and

Mural Tablet of John Law

ordered learning that both gives the poem its individual character and makes it so typically Elizabethan. Just so Pope's *Rape of the Lock* unites the solid doctrine of good sense with the fashionable elegances of an artificial society. Davies wrote less carefully than Pope, but the two poems stand in a similar relation to their respective ages.

The solidity of the subject-matter can best be conveyed by a short summary of the poem's evolution. One night when Penelope at Ithaca appeared among her suitors, Athena inspired her with special beauty. Antinous, most courtly of the suitors, begs her to imitate the motions of the heavens by joining in a dance. There follows a regular disputation on the subject of dancing: Antinous upholding its virtue at great length, Penelope interposing brief condemnations of it. Antinous's arguments are arranged in a careful sequence. The dance is the order which in the beginning creative Love imposed on a formless universe. Love harmonised the elements into an orderly dance. He created the "gods' eternal bower" and the starry heavens. Enchanted with this heavenly order, he is shocked to see the disorder prevailing among the newly created inhabitants of earth. He descends and calling them into a circle expounds in a long speech the orderly dances that are proceeding in the entire universe. The fixed stars the planets and the elements below the planets have their dances. On earth, lowest of the elements, the streams the flowers and the animals have their proper dances also. Such is Love's lesson; and it leads to Antinous's exposition of the dance in human society. All order in peace and war is a dance: so are the seven liberal arts. And when Penelope objects, Antinous retorts that she herself is full of the dance without knowing it and that the very disposition of her household has the dance's order. Antinous has ranged through the whole universe ending in man and his social organisation. There still remains the political order. But this is differently introduced. Finding Penelope unconvinced Antinous prays Love himself to help him. Love appears and gives him a magic mirror. This he presents to Penelope, who sees in it a vision of the moon surrounded by the dancing stars, or Queen Elizabeth watching her courtiers dancing "in this our Golden Age". This dance, symbolising the orderly disposition of the body politic, completes Davies's survey of the universe. It would also have persuaded Penelope, if he had finished the poem, to yield to Antinous's prayer.

Such is the substance of *Orchestra*; and, though the opening is striking and diverting, the debate itself is heavy with the matter of the encyclopedias. It is only a powerful lyrical momentum that can animate such matter, just as Shaw needed the most accomplished dramatic technique to float the amount of doctrine contained in many of his plays. Antinous's speech extending from the end of Cupid's reported harangue in stanza 60 to Penelope's rejoinder in stanza 97 is indeed too long drawn out; but otherwise Davies does succeed by the vitality of his fantasy and by the spontaneous variety of his verse in turning what could be flat commonplace either into something amusing and paradoxical or into a sincere criticism of life.

For fantasy take stanza 53:

> *Of all their ways I love Meander's path,*
> *Which to the tunes of dying swans doth dance.*
> *Such winding sleights, such turns and tricks he hath,*
> *Such creeks, such wrenches, and such dalliance,*
> *That, whether it be hap or heedless chance,*
> *In his indented course and wriggling play*
> *He seems to dance a perfect cunning hay.*

The matter is the stalest schoolboy stock: the windings of Meander, the covert reference to Homer, past whose reputed tomb the Meander flowed, the swan-song. Yet by sheer wealth of vocabulary, by an ingenuous exhibition of saying the same things in different and startling ways and by adding a twist of sheer outrageousness to the stalely mythological, he succeeds. What could be fresher than *indented course* or *wriggling play*? and yet they come out of the bottom of the bag. And what more nonsensical than the notion of the waters of the Meander keeping time with their unbroken flow to the defunctive music of large numbers of the *Cycnus Asiaticus*? But Davies is so gay, so certain of not being gainsaid that the reader is forced to agree that the Meander (although neither party has seen it) is the best of all rivers. Henryson had described the bravery of youth surpassingly well in the lament of Cresseid, but he describes it from without in verse that is not conspicuously youthful. Davies deals mainly with the accumulated doctrines of many ages yet in rhythms that embody youthful vitality.

> *Love in the twinkling of your eyelids danceth,*
> *Love danceth in your pulses and your veins,*
> *Love, when you sew, your needle's point advanceth*
> *And makes it dance a thousand curious strains*
> *Of winding rounds, whereof the form remains,*
> *To show that your fair hands can dance the hay,*
> *Which your fine feet would learn as well as they.*

The very iteration of *Love* here is like the beat of a young, full-blooded pulse.

One of the poem's charms is the easy rapid conversational accent that accompanies the fantasy. In stanza 6 he tells us that he intends to sing "a plain and easy melody"; and so, as far as lucid sense and unaffected cadences go, he does. But it is the paradoxical crossing of such simplicity with a high-wrought imagination that gives pleasure. The very next stanza will illustrate.

> *Only one night's discourse I can report:*
> *When the great torchbearer of heaven was gone*
> *Down, in a mask, unto the Ocean's court,*
> *To revel it with Tethys all alone,*
> *Antinous, disguised and unknown,*
> *Like to the spring in gaudy ornament,*
> *Unto the castle of the princess went.*

This is indeed a plain and easy melody, yet how beautifully it shows up the gorgeous periphrasis of the falling of night.

c

33

But Davies has other examples of variety. Fantasy can give way to strong imagination, and charm to majesty. For strong imagination take stanza 49.

> *For lo, the sea, that fleets about the land*
> *And like a girdle clips her solid waist,*
> *Music and measure both doth understand;*
> *For his great crystal eye is always cast*
> *Up to the moon and on her fixed fast;*
> *And as she danceth in her pallid sphere,*
> *So danceth he about the centre here.*

To talk of the sea's *great crystal eye* is more than fancy. The comparison between the vast sea and the small human feature, at first sight surprising in a trivial way, is yet ratified by the reason. The shape of both is curved; both offer surfaces for reflected light; both have their little-known and important depths beneath those surfaces. Even the actual vision of the moon reflected in the sea is summoned up. Deep feelings have been aroused. In passing let me note that Davies's comparison is in the Metaphysical manner, but thrown out with an ease and then cast away with a tact which the Metaphysicals themselves do not always command.

For majesty take two culminating points. In stanza 96 Antinous completes his main survey of the universe and the way the dance rules throughout it. In 97 Penelope makes her longest retort. And in 102 Antinous gathers himself together for his most solemn argument: the great God of Love, oldest of the gods and the world's creator, must not be confused with the profane god of the same name.

> *Yet once again Antinous did reply:*
> *Great queen, condemn not Love the innocent*
> *For this mischievous Lust, which traitorously*
> *Usurps his name and steals his ornament;*
> *For that true Love, which dancing did invent,*
> *Is he that tun'd the world's whole harmony*
> *And link'd all men in sweet society.*

He first extracted from th' earth-mingled mind
That heavenly fire or quintessence divine
Which doth such sympathy in beauty find
As is between the elm and fruitful vine,
And so to beauty ever doth incline;
Life's life it is, and cordial to the heart,
And of our better part the better part.

And Davies goes on to the wonderful stanzas, one of which I quoted above, about Love dancing in Penelope without her knowing it. The second place is the description of the English court, as he himself shows when in stanza 127 he breaks off to invoke Urania in place of Terpsichore. He never wrote his description of Queen Elizabeth, but his description of the court justifies his invocation.

Her brighter dazzling beams of majesty
Were laid aside, for she vouchsaf'd awhile
With gracious cheerful and familiar eye
Upon the revels of her court to smile;
For so time's journeys she doth oft beguile.
Like sight no mortal eye might elsewhere see
So full of art state and variety.

By speaking of majesty I did not mean to imply that *Orchestra* is a great poem. In intensity of feeling it falls short of the *Testament of Cresseid* and is nearer to the third poem, Dryden's *Ode on Mrs Killigrew*. It is also less closely wrought than either of these. It is a "lucky" poem; careless in parts: yet we overlook or forgive the carelessness because of the animation. It is a generous poem, making us feel mean if we niggle over details. Lastly it is an impudent poem; but we let the impudence ramp us, for we know it is the impudence of youth not of ingrained character.

The matters so far dealt with are all such as would apply to the literature of any age. If the reader agrees that they make *Orchestra* a delightful poem we can read and re-read, he should be ready to consider what things in the poem are the special marks of the Elizabethan age.

II

(a)

MOTION AND FIXITY

Orchestra is a poem on dancing and should therefore suggest motion. But the motion suggested has a wider reference. If the deliberation of Henryson's verse matched the repose bred by the universal acceptance of certain large ideas, the dynamic quality of Davies's verse proclaims a delight in new experience and in enlarged horizons. It implies the context of the Elizabethan voyages of discovery: indeed the whole frame of mind the classic expression of which is Tamburlaine's speech about nature, having framed us of four elements, teaching us to have aspiring minds. The final stanza about the Indians

With pearl and painted plumes themselves adorning,

although derivative, is more than casual ornament, like Milton's references to Ormuz and Ind, which had behind them a strong contemporary concern with overland routes to the Persian Gulf and India. Antinous, however much he is represented as the perfection of knightly courtesy, is self-assured and cheeky in a manner very different from the Troilus either of Chaucer or of Henryson. He is the adventurer, in whatever sense, rather than the knight with all the limiting duties of knighthood. A Marxist critic would readily (and not without some justification) see him as the new type of speculator, the man who organised or financed or took part in the new commercial and explorative companies. Certainly he is a very efficient salesman of dancing. A comparison may here help. Elyot in his *Book of the Governor* has a long section on dancing and its educative value. He is just as concerned as Davies to propagate the excellences of the art. Indeed, there are so many resemblances that Elyot may well be the main

36

source of Davies's poem. This, however, is irrelevant to
the differences of tone. Elyot, it must be allowed, is writing
didactic prose, but even so the difference between his careful compilation of arguments and the impetus catching up
and informing all Davies's many details is very striking.
There may be new matter in Elyot, but his disposition is
nearer Henryson's. The following passage gives a fair
notion of his method of argument:

Now because there is no pastime to be compared to that wherein
may be founden both recreation and meditation of virtue, I
have among all honest pastimes wherein is exercise of the body
noted dancing to be of an excellent utility, comprehending in it
wonderful figures, or as the Greeks do call them *Ideae*, of virtues
and noble qualities, and specially of the commodious virtue
called prudence, whom Tully defineth to be the knowledge of
things which ought to be desired and followed and also of them
which ought to be fled from or eschewed. . . . This virtue being
so commodious to man, and as it were the porch of the noble
palace of man's reason, whereby all other virtues shall enter, it
seemeth to me right expedient that, as soon as opportunity may
be founden, a child or young man be thereto induced. And because that the study of virtue is tedious for the more part to
them that do flourish in young years, I have devised how in the
form of dancing, now late used in this realm among gentlemen,
the whole description of this virtue, prudence, may be founden
out and well perceived as well by the dancers as by them which
standing by will be diligent beholders and markers. . . . The first
moving in every dance is called "honour", which is a reverent
inclination or curtsy with a long deliberation or pause and is
but one motion comprehending the time of three other motions
or setting forth of the foot. By that may be signified that at the
beginning of all our acts we should do due honour to God,
which is the root of prudence; which honour is compact of
three things, fear love and reverence: and that in the beginning
of all things we should advisedly with some tract of time behold
and foresee the success of our enterprise.[1]

[1] Book i, chap. 22.

And Elyot goes on with great deliberation to moralise all the other figures of the dance. And the result is static, enumerative not emotional, an arithmetical not a geometrical progression.

But it would be as superficial to confine the temper of *Orchestra* to mere motion as to confine its style to unmitigated fantasy. Davies did not write his religious poem, *Nosce Teipsum*, till later, yet the content of that poem is one of the presuppositions to which *Orchestra* is adjusted. Hooker's picture of God's Law in the first book of *Laws of Ecclesiastical Polity* is at once contemporary and entirely alive. And it is in outline the picture [1] Henryson and his contemporaries took for granted and Davies inserted, with individual embellishment, in *Orchestra*.

The fundamentally religious nature of this picture was mentioned on p. 28 above. When it came to details, the Elizabethans regarded the world organisation under three figures: a chain, a set of correspondences, and a dance. The chain, of inconceivable magnitude, began with the Seraph nearest God's throne and extended in descending order of magnitude through every cosmic item to the meanest scrap of inanimate matter, man being the link between the intellectual and the bestial creation. The second figure was horizontal: a series of superimposed but corresponding planes. The order of God in heaven with the angelic hierarchies was the highest plane, the political order with a king at the head was another, the sea containing within it duplicates of whatever existed on land another, the microcosm of man with his hierarchies of faculties, physical and mental, another still. No cosmic item lacked its place in one of these departments. Finally, there is the figure of the universe as one great dance with every item taking its appropriate part: an idea not less hierarchical or closely knit than the other two but substituting a kaleidoscopic for a static design.

Davies, in choosing the third figure by which to express

[1] This picture is the theme of my *Elizabethan World Picture*, to which I refer the reader for further detail.

his world picture, implies the other two, and in so doing he is the authentic spokesman of his age. Writing, like Henryson, in pagan guise he omits the angels from the chain, but when Cupid preaches his sermon to the rout of men he does describe natural creation in an order that implies the chain's sequence. He begins with the highest heavenly bodies, the fixed stars, goes on to the planets, then to the elements situated between the moon and the earth, then to the inhabitants and materials of the earth itself. And if here he departs from the chain's order, putting vegetables and minerals before man, he does so for structural reasons, for he wishes to lead up to man and to come to rest on his political organisation. To the various correspondences there are many references. First, the whole poem is constructed on the correspondences between the dance of the heavenly bodies, the dance in the sea and earthly creation, the dance in the body politic typified by Elizabeth's court, and the human motion of dancing to which Penelope is invited. And there are many striking details. Elizabeth and her courtiers correspond respectively to the Moon in her full majesty and the other less bright stars. In stanzas 62 and 63 Davies is impelled to seek a correspondence with the whole turn at the end of a dance figure and he finds it in the final circular motion of a stream, which, after having gone this way and that like the dancers in the body of the dance, ends by moving in the unbroken revolution of the ocean. In stanza 68 the physical leaps into the air that occur in the galliard correspond to the mind's aspiration after heaven. This last correspondence is the most fantastic of all, but it is none the less Elizabethan. And it can be paralleled for fantasy in a famous contemporary passage. Theseus's hounds in *A Midsummer Night's Dream* were

> *Slow in pursuit but match'd in mouth like bells*
> *Each under each.*

Theseus's hounds were not unique, for there is other evidence that some Elizabethan sportsmen chose their hounds so that their notes made an octave, a quire as well as a pack. And the reason for so doing was not a mere piece of picturesqueness, of unrelated fantasy. A main point of such hounds was that they contributed to the design of the universe by duplicating in the animal world the heavenly music of the spheres.

But the great thing about *Orchestra* is neither the dynamic force nor the great unchanging traditional background. It is rather the union of the two, the ability to have it both ways. And this wonderful ability was the mark of the Elizabethan age generally. In the background is the grand outline of the medieval world picture; in the foreground is the inquiring and eager temper set off and enhanced by the picture it is ultimately destined to destroy. The significant stanza is 51, which reposes on the old Ptolemaic astronomy but mentions, oblivious of danger, the conjectures of Copernicus:

> *Only the earth doth stand forever still:*
> *Her rocks remove not, nor her mountains meet;*
> *(Although some wits enrich'd with learning's skill*
> *Say heaven stands firm and that the earth doth fleet*
> *And swiftly turneth underneath their feet)*
> *Yet, though the earth is ever steadfast seen,*
> *On her broad breast hath dancing ever been.*

It is no exaggeration to talk about danger: men believed axiomatically in the coherence of the universe and the mutual interdependence of all its parts; and an axiom is not upset without the danger of violent repercussions. This passage near the end of Castiglione's *Courtier* is typical of the common belief.

Behold the state of this great engine of the world, which God created for the health and preservation of every thing that was made. The heaven round beset with so many heavenly lights; and in the middle the earth environed with the elements and upheld with the weight of itself; the sun, that compassing about giveth light to the whole and in winter season draweth to the lowermost sign, afterward by little and little climbeth again to the other part; the moon, that of him taketh her light according as she draweth nigh or goeth farther from him; and the other five stars, that diversely keep the very same course. These things among themselves have such force by the knitting together of an order so necessarily framed that with altering them any one jot they should all be loosed and the world would decay.

And Copernicus was not the only man who had given a danger signal. Nevertheless, though here and there an Elizabethan might tremble for the security of the accepted universe, in general the pains of severe reorientation were postponed till the seventeenth century; and the magnificent stanza (36) in which Cupid reassures his audience that the seeming disorder of the stars is unreal does indeed represent the Elizabethan confidence:

> *What if to you these sparks disorder'd seem,*
> *As if by chance they had been scatter'd there?*
> *The gods a solemn measure do it deem*
> *And see a just proportion everywhere*
> *And know the points whence first their movings were,*
> *To which first points when all return again,*
> *The axletree of heaven shall break in twain.*

One reason for this confidence will be found in the next section.

(b)

THE BODY POLITIC

Although in general outline the world pictures as imagined by Henryson and Davies were the same, they differed in one important particular: the body politic is much more prominent in Davies. When he brings *Orchestra* to rest on the great description of the Mortal Moon turning her gracious eye on her courtiers dancing he neither indulges a merely private fantasy nor is he cynically seeking a job at court through personal flattery: he is being sincere; and in his sincerity he implies both a

41

change in the status of the monarchy since Henryson's day and a new kind of political pride. The body politic with its head, usually a king, had been a part of the traditional, religiously conceived, world order. And as an important part of it the king had his share of sanctity, but the position of Elizabeth was different. With the rise of nationalism in the fifteenth century, with the successful despotism of the Tudors, with the transference to the monarchy of ultimate ecclesiastical authority, the English throne usurped a portion of the awe formerly possessed by the religious organisation. Secondly, the Tudors had, unbelievably, not only rescued England from civil war, but had continued to keep her clear of it. Germany, in their time, had suffered a terrible revolt of the peasants, France had been torn by religious conflict: in wonderful contrast England had not only kept internal peace, had not only rested true to herself, but had grown far more conscious of her own nature, had, as it were, found herself. That a modern would have been ill at ease in the brutality and turbulence of much Elizabethan life and that many Elizabethans were fiercely critical of contemporary manners do not alter these facts; facts which declare themselves through the assured tone of Davies's culminating description of the English court. But it must not be forgotten that this description comes within the context of the total world picture. The Elizabethans really saw their queen as part of the great divine scheme. And contrariwise the political stability of Elizabeth was that scheme's defence against the new ideas that threatened its existence.

Davies never wrote his description of Elizabeth, but in tone it would surely have resembled many other descriptions, for instance Spenser's in the *Fairy Queen* under the guise of Belphoebe or Lyly's in *Euphues and his England*. They make strange reading to-day and can easily be misunderstood. They sound wildly extravagant and remote from truth. But in actual fact they imply neither insincerity nor a defective grasp of things as they are. It should be plain that the Elizabethans enthusiastically prized

something that had come to rest in the person of Elizabeth. At the same time they were very practical people and
could have had no illusions about her character as an
ordinary woman. It is precisely this co-existence of the
idealising faculty with a strong practical sense which was
so characteristically Elizabethan and which some moderns
find difficult to believe possible. That an Elizabethan
gentleman could have undertaken a desperate voyage both
in the spirit of Mallory on his Everest expedition and of
an eighteenth century slave-trader they find difficult to
credit; or that Shakespeare could have combined the dis-
interested activity of the visionary with a regard to the
takings of the box office. If they are to understand the
Elizabethans they must not only credit but expect such
combinations: of which Davies's authorship of *Orchestra*
and his success in the practical sphere of the law is yet
another.[1]

(c)

PLATONISM

The Platonism of *Orchestra* is found in stanzas 102 to
108, where Antinous speaks of the nature of Penelope's
beauty. And I must now ask the reader to turn them up in
a text. They merit careful reading for they are a precise
expression of a precise yet transcendental doctrine. Penelope has just condemned not only dancing but Love, who
was dancing's parent. Antinous replies that she is con-
founding Love with Lust. Lust counterfeits the attributes
of Love; but it was Love, the author of the world's harmony and of the social sense in man, who truly created
dancing (stanza 102). But Love did more. He separated
the divine spark in man from the shackles of the sensual
element in him and inclined it to the Platonic idea of the
Beautiful. This divine spark is the very life of our life
(stanza 103). The next stanza is more difficult to interpret,

[1] I have dealt more fully with Elizabethan conception of history in my
Shakespeare's History Plays, pp. 59-70, 142-5.

first because there are now two gods of Love (and both of them virtuous), Cupid and his son, Love, and secondly because, for a moment, the conventional Petrarchian notion of the hard-hearted lady is interposed into the Platonism. But the meaning seems to be as follows: Corresponding to the divine spark in man is the true spirit of love which informs and dances through every part of Penelope, her heart excepted. (Her heart is excepted, first because the Petrarchian lady was conventionally heartless and secondly because the true Platonic love belonged to a higher region of the microcosm than the heart, namely to the highest faculty of the brain.) The thought is developed in the next stanza (105). Beauty is simply the dance which the love god performs in the different parts of Penelope's microcosm. And the next two stanzas elaborate this dance. Finally (stanza 108) there is the dance in Penelope's soul, where all the virtues move in the circular motion of heaven. This, we are meant to understand, is akin to the angelic; and if Antinous could see it he would be overcome and cast into a trance.

Such is the content of these stanzas and it presupposes a knowledge of the theories of Platonic love current in the Renaissance. These theories are both like and unlike the relations between courtly love and orthodox religion mentioned in the last chapter. The religious assumption was behind them both, and it is a great mistake to think that the Renaissance vogue of Platonic love was anti-Christian and a reversion to paganism. A second resemblance is that in both schemes sensual love was a means to a religious end. But there are great differences. First, the ideal religious end of courtly love was monastic, but of Platonic love, mystical. Secondly, courtly love was bad in itself and led to religion only through its by-products, of which fidelity was the best; in contrast Platonic love was not a false step, something to be gone back on, but a bridge or a stair, good as far as it went but leading farther or higher. In the Platonic scheme, sensual love was the first step of the stair; and it became bad only if the aspirant, whose business it was to climb, remained stationary. Then indeed it became bad and caused chaos and misery of mind, and any use it had was the lesson of experience. Warned by the misery to which purely sensual love led, a man might step down from the first stair and then later resume his pilgrimage with a better chance of success. The actual stair was an ascent from sensuality to the non-sensual love of the individual, to the love of sexual beauty generally, and at last to an essential beauty from which sex had quite disappeared. The sensual feeling was discarded gradually and was bad only if the discarding process was interfered with. A kiss was a legitimate stage in the process, for as well as the meeting of lips it was the fusion of souls. The ascent of the stair was difficult. Only a few superior people were able to achieve it, and the danger of relapsing into sensuality was recognised.

Antinous's words to Penelope mean that she is exceptionally well qualified to be the instrument of the Platonic ascent. Her bodily beauty is the perfect index of her beauty of soul and is well calculated both to attract the lover initially and to draw him up through the preliminary stages.

Davies here represents an important and wide-spread phase of Elizabethan thought and the one most difficult for a modern to be at ease with. It continues medieval habits of thought in being essentially religious, but it is a genuine innovation of the Renaissance in being a part of humanism: holiness through, and not in spite of, the human. The most authoritative popular statement of the doctrine was Bembo's long discourse at the end of the fourth book of Castiglione's *Courtier*, so widely read by the Elizabethans in Hoby's translation. One of its finest expositions is Spenser's *Four Hymns*, and the most interesting example of it in action is Sidney's love for Stella. The experience recorded in *Astrophel and Stella* is real, the poem is certainly not the poetising of a correctly imagined conventional love-affair. But its reality is not that of the ordinary entanglement in which a man gets involved heedlessly or involuntarily. It is rather a Platonic experiment deliberately entered on. The sonnets themselves describe an early stage of the process, when sense is still powerful, and only hints at the higher amatory education. But when at the end Sidney tells the love that reaches but to dust to leave him and invokes eternal love to fill the gap, he is writing platonically.

The Elizabethan devotion to Platonic love is one more example of their resolute idealism, the two already mentioned being the spirit of adventure and the exaltation of Queen Elizabeth. And like these it is united with a hard sense of real life. It would have troubled an Elizabethan much less than a modern if a man was both far advanced in the process of Platonic love and at the same time satisfied the simple craving of the senses in a simple way: provided of course the persons concerned were kept rigidly distinct. Similarly an Elizabethan would have found little difficulty with the current Platonic doctrine that a beautiful mind inhabits a beautiful body and its apparent inaccuracy in real life. Here is Spenser's exposition:

> So every spirit, as it is most pure,
> And hath in it the more of heavenly light,
> So it the fairer body doth procure
> To habit in and it more fairly dight
> With cheerful grace and amiable sight:
> For of the soul the body form doth take,
> For soul is form and doth the body make.
>
> Yet oft it falls that many a gentle mind
> Dwells in deformed tabernacle drown'd
> Either by chance against the course of kind
> Or through unaptness in the substance found,
> Which it assumed of some stubborn ground
> That will not yield unto her form's direction
> But is perform'd with some foul imperfection.
>
> And oft it falls (ay me, the more to rue!)
> That goodly beauty, allbe heavenly born,
> Is foul abus'd.[1]

[1] *An Hymn in Honour of Beauty*, 127-33, 141-50.

ORCHESTRA

It was the strength of the Elizabethans that they did not allow their sense of reality to break their belief in their ideal and that some of them strove to shape their acts on that ideal's model.

(d)

EDUCATION

In writing *Orchestra* Davies had no conscious educational intent but he gives abundant signs of the belief in education that was one of the great marks of the Renaissance. The form of the poem is that of the medieval debate and there was nothing exclusively educative about this. But the disputation was the regular educational instrument at the Universities, and with the now wider practice of university residence among the ruling classes the disputation form would tend to be more allied to education. Apart from this Antinous tries to impart to Penelope, already very accomplished, yet one more accomplishment, while the episode of Love gathering his barbaric audience in a ring and instructing them in the constitution of the universe does indeed take for granted the profound Renaissance belief in "nurture".

Once again we must both compare and contrast with the medieval habit of mind. The *Testament of Cresseid* is also an educative poem, but the lesson is in holiness not in knowledge. The Middle Ages certainly held great clerks in reverence but more as prodigies than as prime benefactors. Education in holiness was through the discipline of the flesh and the exercise of the faculties of the mind nearest to the angelic. Man was allied both to the beasts and to the angels: to the beasts through his senses, to the angels through his capacity for contemplation. But he had also the specifically human capacity of learning. The Middle Ages generally put the emphasis on his lower and higher affinities. Now the innovation of the Renaissance was not to question the end of learning accepted by the

47

Middle Ages but to alter the emphasis on the means; and Milton was speaking for the whole of that age when he wrote in his tract *Of Education* as follows:

> The end then of learning is to repair the ruins of our first parents by regaining to know God aright and out of that knowledge to love him, to imitate him, to be like him, as we may the nearest by possessing our souls of true virtue, which being united to the heavenly grace of faith makes up the highest perfection. But because our understanding cannot in this body found itself but on sensible things nor arrive so clearly to the knowledge of God and things invisible as by the orderly conning over the visible and inferior creature, the same method is necessarily to be followed in all discreet teaching.

The end then of education in the eyes of Davies and the Elizabethans was primarily religious but the means was not through the direct striving after things invisible but through the specifically human faculty of learning. In other words man had a better chance of attaining the state of the angels by being the best possible kind of man and exercising the unique human faculty of learning than by a direct imitation of what was specifically the angelic function. It was a happy notion, a union of pagan ethics with Christian orthodoxy: the confidence that by following Aristotle's doctrine that every creature should fulfil its own natural functions you simultaneously qualified for the kingdom of heaven.

And on this note of happiness, so eminently apt to Davies's poem, I end the present section.

Chimney-Piece by Grinling Gibbons

DRYDEN

Ode on Anne Killigrew 1686

I

HENRYSON'S *Testament of Cresseid* is a beautiful and moving poem of one good minor poet; Davies's *Orchestra* a beautiful and exhilarating poem of another. Dryden's *Ode on Anne Killigrew* is a masterpiece of a major poet. We need not like it best, but, if we do compare, it makes the other two look a little amateurish. One reason for this is the high proportion of our attention which, at first sight, the purely formal qualities of the *Ode* usurp. Henryson's tragic story, the setting of *Orchestra* and the world picture and the politics set forth in it, count for more than the purely prose content of the *Ode*. Dryden does indeed tell us things about Anne Killigrew: that she was virtuous and gifted; that she wrote verse and painted landscapes and royal portraits; and that she died of smallpox. But the two hundred lines spent in saying this are, as information, nearly all padding, while what astonishes and delights is the wealth of imaginative invention and the glory of the verbal music. Here, if anywhere, Arnold's attribution of the prosaic to Augustan verse is refuted, while the raptures into which his contemporaries fell over one kind of musical verse are perfectly appropriate to the excellence if not to the kind of Dryden's.

The form of the *Ode* is inherited directly from Cowley, but further ancestry included Spenser's *Epithalamion* and Ben Jonson, while the accent of majesty owes much to Milton and particularly to his short pieces *On Time*, *Upon the Circumcision*, and *At a Solemn Music*. Compare for instance this from Dryden's *Ode*

> *Hear then a mortal Muse thy praise rehearse*
> *In no ignoble verse*

D   49

FIVE POEMS

with this from *On Time*

> *Then long Eternity shall greet our bliss*
> *With an individual kiss.*

The invention and music are not equally brilliant throughout, but I cannot agree with Mark Van Doren that the
Ode is "sadly uneven" and that apart from three great
stanzas the rest are at the most equal to Cowley. In general
the tone of solemn rapture is sustained, and the ebbings
form the preparations, necessary in a long lyric, for the
full flood of music. There may however be isolated lapses.
It is hard to feel warmly about the political metaphor in
stanza six: the idea that through the descriptive passages
in her poetry Anne had staked out claims in the adjacent
province of painting, as an ambitious ruler forms seditious
groups in the country he means to invade.

> *To the next realm she stretched her sway,*
> *For Painture near adjoining lay,*
> *A plenteous province and alluring prey.*
> *A Chamber of Dependences was framed*
> *(As conquerors will never want pretence,*
> *When armed, to justify the offence),*
> *And the whole fief in right of Poetry she claimed.*

And at the end of stanza seven the line

> *What next she had designed, Heaven only knows*

is not impressive in sound even if we can forget the
absurdity which a modern does, and a contemporary did
not, find in it.[1]

After the music the construction calls for admiration.
The poem is an elegy on a poetess and like the Dido poem
in Spenser's *Shepherd's Calendar*, like *Lycidas*, and like
Adonais it presupposes the happy fate of the deceased. It
is built on the two themes of earth and heaven, which
themselves are linked by the commonplace that earthly

---

[1] *Heaven only knows* means in the context that heaven, having heard
her songs there, does know, as mortals cannot, what her next artistic efforts
would have been, had she survived.

poetry partakes of the divine; and it evolves as follows. The first stanza gives the three main themes: poetry, for Anne Killigrew is even now singing; heaven and earth, for she sings in some heavenly region, while her earthly songs served as prelude and probation for the heavenly music. The second stanza has the same mixture of theme but with the emphasis on earth and her pre-natal poetical antecedents. By immediate heredity she comes of poetical stock, by re-incarnation from Sappho. The stanza ends with heaven. Anne Killigrew's is too pure a soul to suffer further incarnation: when she has ceased listening to the poem now addressed to her she must return to the quire of heavenly singers. The third stanza again contains all three themes but with the emphasis on heaven, which celebrated her birth with joy. This pure heavenly rejoicing suggests its contrary in stanza four, the general impurity of contemporary poetry; and the pessimistic satirical and urgent tone contrasts finely with the serene static tone of the first three stanzas. It comes to rest on Anne Killigrew and the thought that she was both an exception and an atonement. In so doing it introduces the body of the ode, stanzas five to eight, which deal with the lady's attainments on earth. Heaven is kept in the background, and we hear of her successes in poetry and in painting and of her untimely death. Death leads to mourning, and in stanza nine her brother's sorrow when he learns the news is conjectured. But he is at sea and has no news. Only, if sailorlike he scans the stars, he might notice a new bright member of the Pleiades—the star which is his sister's soul. This mention of the stars is the return of the theme of heaven; and it leads to the last stanza, where poetry heaven and earth are brought together in the description of the opening graves and the Last Judgement with Anne Killigrew leading the poets, the first souls to join their resurrected bodies, to their heavenly mansion. The poem's evolution is perfect, and it is the greatest pity that in the *Oxford Book of English Verse*, the chief recent means of access, it should have been truncated.

FIVE POEMS

So far I have dealt with matters of forms, and it may now be asked of what feelings, opinions, or states of mind are the poem's music and formal perfection the index.

The states of mind poems express stand at varying distances from the subjects these poems purport to treat. Dryden's subject, Anne Killigrew's premature death, has no close connection with the things he was really saying. He must have known that her poems and pictures were the indifferent stuff which posterity has decided them to be. Nevertheless he used the conventional grief and extravagant adulation to convey certain strongly held opinions and feelings.

One of these is a heartfelt enthusiasm for the arts, the same enthusiasm that animates Dryden's literary criticism. When he praises Anne Killigrew's accomplishment, he is speaking not for her but for poetry and painting in their entirety; and when at the end he makes the earth lie more lightly on the poets than on other men, he is paying a sincere tribute to the poetic sensibility: a tribute not less sincere for the outrageous assertion that Anne Killigrew will lead the poetic throng to heaven. There is no piety in his references to heavenly music, yet through them he demonstrates how sincerely he prizes the practice of the arts on this earth.

Next, by attributing to Anne Killigrew many excellences which she did not possess and by putting that attribution into a shapely form Dryden expressed his belief in manners and decorum. Decorum is connected with what should be, not with what is. We regulate the opening and the end of our letters on that principle. And Dryden attributed to the object of his elegy the qualities it was proper for her to have, whether or not she did in fact have them.

Both the above beliefs belong to a more general one which we can call a belief in civilisation and which includes the beliefs in solid craft against empty ingenuity, in reason against fanaticism, in order against disorder, in monarchy against mob-rule, in established religion against arbitrary and undisciplined nonconformity. Some of these beliefs could be substantiated from the details of the poem. For instance the single line in stanza five

Each test and every light her Muse will bear

testifies to the belief in solid craft. But the most powerful expression is of the general principle, and it is given by the very movement and composition of the poem: by the controlled yet enthusiastic movement, by the masterly formal and logical shape, and by the nobly pompous circumlocutions.

Born to the spacious empire of the Nine—

the accent of that implies social and political order.

If even a portion of the above claims is accepted the *Ode* is found to possess a substance that answers worthily to those formal and musical qualities that first strike us. It takes its rank among the major elaborate lyrics such as the opening odes in the third book of Horace.

II

Most of the matters just enumerated have a direct bearing on the general thought of the age. I therefore can now pass easily from speaking of Dryden's *Ode* as a work of art to the ideas which it embodies.

(*a*)

THE WORLD PICTURE

Many of the things which I said Dryden stood for would have been accepted by other ages. Certainly, Henryson and Davies believed in order and decorum. What then distinguishes Dryden's belief from theirs? It is not a question of mere knowledge. Dryden knows all about order and degree and the "vast chain of being"; he still inherits the medieval scheme of the universe. His account of the various regions of the eternal heavens where the soul of Anne Killigrew might inhabit is as precise as anything in *Orchestra*. She has left the regions of mutability below the moon; she may be in a planet (comparatively close to the earth); she may be in the region of the fixed stars and circle with the great host of heaven; or she may be called to "more superior bliss", farther from earth and nearer to God, in the empyrean. Similarly with the stars: he knows about their conjunctions and horoscopes. He uses the technical term *in trine* when he says that the more malicious stars (like Saturn and Mars) were in a benign mood at Anne Killigrew's birth. Along with this correctness is the orthodoxy of the last stanza. Anne Killigrew, now in heaven, will reassume her body on the Day of Judgement and reascend to her final heavenly home. It looks as if the old material were there; and yet the emphasis has altered, being now on man and off the rest of creation in a new way. In other words the humanism of the Renaissance, which in Davies was still truly combined with the inherited world picture, has been carried much further and has destroyed the old proportions. Dryden really believes in the social virtues of human civilisation, but he does not really believe in astrology (as the "advanced" men of his age did not believe in it) nor in the angels. In fact he uses both stars and angels primarily as ornaments. The address of Anne Killigrew as a "young probationer and candidate of heaven" is charming, even impressive, in its context but it is an ornamental conceit not a conceit containing the genuine belief that she was in the act of ascending the ladder of creation into the angelic state. Walton in his biography of Hooker describes him on his deathbed

> meditating the number and nature of the angels and their blest obedience and order, without which peace would not be in heaven; and oh that it might be so on earth.

Of course Hooker was a divine, but even so he lived in a different world from Dryden's. His vision of cosmic order is a grander if stranger imagining than Dryden's eminently human principle of ornamental decorum. Then take the lower end of the chain of being: the animals and inanimate nature. One of Anne Killigrew's pictures takes these in.

> *The sylvan scenes of herds and flocks*
> *And fruitful plains and barren rocks;*
> *Of shallow brooks that flowed so clear,*
> *The bottom did the top appear;*
> *Of deeper too and ampler floods,*
> *Which as in mirrors show'd the woods;*
> *Of lofty trees, with sacred shades*
> *And perspectives of pleasant glades,*
> *Where nymphs of brightest form appear*
> *And shaggy satyrs standing near,*
> *Which them at once admire and fear.*

This is purely descriptive and ornamental. There is not the least sense of any of the things pictured being a part of a cosmic as against a decorative scene. Nymphs and satyrs are simple classical ornament, they are not the classical equivalent of "real" supernatural beings with their necessary place in the chain. The same is true of the herds and flocks. Nor is there any sense of the landscape being emblematic or of corresponding to any other cosmic plane. Anything that is not purely pictorial is realistic, looking forward to the nature-poetry of Thomson, to the age of science and away from the age of theology.

It could not be otherwise. The doubts about the world order, present yet pending in the age of Elizabeth, had been realised. The heavens had proved to be not immutable, the earth was no longer the centre of creation, and the political stability of the Tudors, which had done so much to conserve the framework of the old order, had given way to a less popular house and to civil war. With the beginnings of science it was the facts and not the supposed perfect organisation of the physical world that excited men's imaginations. And the exploitation of those facts was man's affair and not God's. A new adjustment was necessary, and it was at the expense of the two extremes of the chain of being.

The theological effects of this change in the scale came out in the next century. Dryden's age was one of great nominal piety. In believing less in the angels it did not intend to believe less in God. But by believing more exclusively in man it did prepare for a theological change. When there was a continuous chain of existence up to the foot of God's throne, God, though inconceivably remote, was directly linked with man. When the intervening links were snapped, there might remain other means of access, yet the suggestion arose that God was somehow less concerned with his creation than before. Those who had no very lively sense of the single soul's direct communication with its God would tend to sever communication altogether. Hence the Deism of the eighteenth century with its idea of a God, perfectly benevolent indeed, but who had created once and for all a world so satisfactory that further interference by him was unnecessary. Dryden would have repudiated such heresy, but by his accent when he writes of the angels and the lower creation he was really preparing the way for it.

(b)

DECORUM

Dryden's *Ode* implies a strong agreement with the contemporary estimation of manners and decorum. It offers a splendid pompous façade and in so doing protests that a good outward show is self-valuable. In stanza seven the king and queen are described in terms of what ideally they should be, not as they were, and Dryden has perfect assurance that he is right to speak thus. We may perceive this assurance the better, if, in contrast, we speculate on the state of mind of the *Times* reporter who in describing the coronation of Edward VII wrote quite blatantly and in cool prose that the noblest looking figure in the Abbey was the King. It was surely very different from Dryden's when he wrote

> *In beauty foremost, as in rank, the queen.*

Given the times he lived in, Dryden really had no choice but to write like that: anything else, in a formal ode, would be scandalously ill-mannered. Any compulsion the *Times* reporter experienced was a smaller and more commercial matter; and we can hope that as he wrote he felt a sinking of the heart or a touch of nausea. For a second example of decorum take the lardscape in stanza six. Though it may be vivid and though some of the details may recall actual nature, it is above all what a landscape should be: a staged piece after the manner of Claude; decorous above everything.

It is worth comparing this sense of decorum with the incident of changing the tapestries mentioned above (p. 28). There too decorum entered in, but more profoundly. The medieval sense of decorum was of course partly superstitious—it would be unlucky to make peace in a place hung with warlike tapestries—but it went beyond mere human manners to the whole nature of the world. The Augustan sense of decorum concerned human manners and social life, and did not go beyond these.

This emphasis on manners must have gained strength from the recent contacts with France. The French have felt and still do feel more strongly than the Anglo-Saxons about the value of manners irrespectively of what they express or conceal. The contrasted tempers are well brought out in Henry James's *American* in the episode where the hero's French friend is hanging between life and death after a duel. The preparations, physical sentimental and spiritual, for death have been made with perfect completeness and propriety, and a second Frenchman is made to remark that with everything so well arranged it would be a pity if death did not ensue. Henry James's American does not sympathise, but a contemporary of Dryden would have understood. The American thought the Frenchman insincere and heartless, the Frenchman thought the American barbaric. Similarly modern readers dislike Restoration literature for being merely formal, a façade with no true feeling behind it, while Restoration readers were shocked by any display of naked feeling. Such displays were found in the Miracle Plays and in the medieval ballad and were thought uncivilised or, as they put it, Gothic. It should be possible to admit the claims of both habits of mind: to admire both the emotional sincerity of *Clerk Saunders* and the genuine moral discipline which any high standard of decorum cannot fail to imply.

There is another form of decorum. When Dryden says he is praising the reception of Anne Killigrew to heaven "in no ignoble verse", he implies the doctrine of decorum governing the different literary kinds. There was an appropriate style for the various subjects. The heavenly theme must be answered by a high manner. It is a principle that explains why Milton used so rough a metre in writing on Hobson and why in *Paradise Lost* he cultivated a sustained manner of writing remote from the chatter of fireside or marketplace. The whole principle is well illustrated by Dryden's last paragraph of his preface to *Religio Laici*, in which he explains why he writes in the style he has chosen.

> The expression of a poem designed purely for instruction ought to be plain and natural and yet majestic; for here the poet is presumed to be a kind of lawgiver, and those three qualities I have named are proper to the legislative style. The florid elevated and figurative way is for the passions.

The same notion of decorum extended to the portrayal of character. Just as Dryden's queen *must* be the most beautiful lady present at the coronation, so any person represented must bear the ideal qualities of his station or profession. Rymer in his *Tragedies of the Last Age* attacked Evadne in Beaumont and Fletcher's *Maid's Tragedy* for her immodesty. The play was a tragedy and it is decorous that all women in tragedy, whatever their conduct, should be naturally modest.

> Tragedy cannot represent a woman without modesty as natural and essential to her. If a woman has got any accidental historical impudence, if, documented in the school of Nanna or Heloisa, she is furnished with some stock of acquired impudence, she is no longer to stalk in tragedy on her high shoes but must rub off and pack down with the carriers into the province of comedy, there to be kicked about and exposed to laughter.

Similarly in his *Short View of Tragedy* Rymer attacked Shakespeare's Iago.

> But what is most intolerable is Iago. He is no blackamoor soldier, so we may be sure he should be like other soldiers of our acquaintance. Yet never in tragedy, nor in comedy, nor in nature, was a soldier with his character. Take it in the author's own words:
>
> > Em.   . . . *some eternal villain,*
> > *Some busy and insinuating rogue,*
> > *Some cogging, cozening slave, to get some office.*
>
> Horace describes a soldier otherwise:
>
> > *Impiger, iracundus, inexorabilis, acer.*
>
> Shakespeare knew his character of Iago was inconsistent . . . but to entertain the audience with something new and surprising, against common sense and nature, he would pass upon us a close, dissembling, false, insinuating rascal instead of an open-hearted frank, plain-dealing soldier, a character constantly worn by them for some thousands of years in the world.

Rymer was an extremist, but the things he pushed to extremes were the things the whole age accepted.

(c)

CLASSICISM

Dryden's poem is highly civilised in a certain way, and it was natural for his contemporaries to look for support to those epochs of history which seemed to be civilised in the same way and to turn against those which seemed hardly civilised at all. In Athens between the times of Pericles and Aristotle and especially in the Rome of Caesar and Augustus human nature and society seemed to be properly prized, superstition properly suppressed, and decorum properly observed, while in the Middle Ages human nature was twisted by asceticism, superstition was rampant, and a fanatical enthusiasm made decorum impossible. Dryden's age knew very much less history than our own. It judged the Periclean and Augustan ages by the acts and opinions of a tiny minority, and it knew nothing of the turn towards humanism about the twelfth century. This ignorance was not all loss, for it enabled the educated class to master a limited area of literature and to get the pleasure that comes from such mastery. This class attained an enviable coherence and uniformity of culture through the assurance that a limited body of knowledge was genuinely common property. Dryden knew that, when in the first stanza of his *Ode* he speculated on the heavenly region where Anne Killigrew's soul might inhabit, every educated reader would know that he was recalling, though in Christian terms, Virgil's speculations at the beginning of the *Georgics* on where the apotheosised Augustus would have his heavenly seat. And it is partly because he is so sure he will be understood that Dryden can take this most daring flight with such steady nerves.

The same passage fulfils too an actual obligation to imitate the classical authors. It was necessary to seek ratification in classical precedent. When Ben Jonson, the first neo-classic critic in England, enjoined *imitation* he meant by it the borrowing and then the moulding of a classical prototype to your own use: in fact what Pope did later in his imitations of Horace. Dryden not only obeys the injunction in the passage just mentioned but by a single touch shows how entirely he approves of it. At the beginning of stanza five he discusses the relation of art and nature in Anne Killigrew's verse.

ODE ON ANNE KILLIGREW

> *Art she had none, yet wanted none,*
> *For Nature did that want supply;*
> *So rich in treasures of her own*
> *She might our boasted stores defy.*
> *Such noble vigour did her verse adorn*
> *That it seemed borrowed, where 'twas only born*

Anne Killigrew's originality, far from being a virtue, needed Dryden's defence. She should have been derivative but luckily she had such native energy that she gave the impression of having borrowed from the classics. The passage is a rough parallel to Pope's elegant fiction in his *Essay on Criticism* of "Young Maro" or Virgil having so strong a native genius as to rely on nature alone. He then turns to Homer (whom he should have copied deliberately) and finds that he has produced something which after all has the appearance of being derived from Homer —and all is well in the end.

(d)

THE STATUS OF THE ARTS

When in the last stanza Dryden speaks of the poets being the first to leave their graves at the Day of Judgement and calls them sacred, he does so in an accent of serene assurance: an assurance lacking in similar pronouncements on the sanctity of poets in Shelley's *Defence of Poetry* and Carlyle's section on the Hero as Poet. Shelley's and Carlyle's protests have the shrillness induced by the knowledge of powerful opposition; Dryden is confident that his words will pass. In an age when scientific truth was threatening the realms of the imagination it is strange that the status of the arts was so high. Yet there is no question that it was so and that it remained so for some years after Dryden's death. One manifestation was the superlative status of the epic among human activities and of epic poets among mortal men. The Earl of Mulgrave in his *Essay upon Poetry*, a poem in couplets published in 1682, was doing nothing unusual when he called Heroic Poems the "chief effort of human sense", and Heroic Poets "gigantic souls" as far above other human beings as an ordinary man is above a changeling. Earlier in the century (1641) in *Reason of Church Government* Milton had said that poetic abilities

> are the inspired gift of God rarely bestowed but yet to some in every nation; and are of power, beside the office of a pulpit, to inbreed and cherish in a great people the seeds of virtue and public civility, to allay the perturbations of the mind and set the affections in right tune:

and Dryden's contemporaries would not have gainsaid him. To recognise that the status of poetry remained high beyond the age of Dryden one can read the list of sub-scribers prefixed to the first edition of Pope's *Iliad* and recall the stories of people pointing him out to their children as the great poet.

How such a state of things was possible is not difficult to perceive. In the Middle Ages poetry had its place either as the handmaiden of religion or as legitimate amusement, but when the hold of the Church over all departments of life was relaxed, some of the awe and glamour possessed by the Church was transferred elsewhere. A part went to the monarchy, a part went to the arts. What had been a craft turned into a fine art; and a craftsman turned into an inspired artist. The process continued into the age of science and actually reached its height in spite of the birth and spread of ideas which, unchecked, would be fatal to the arts. Taken by themselves the ideas animating the newly founded Royal Society were hostile to poetry. Yet Dryden could let his poetic imagination expatiate in his *Ode on Anne Killigrew*, while approving the new scientific activities of the age: a situation not unlike Davies's when he cheerfully included in *Orchestra* his stanza on the Copernican theory, a theory which was destined to destroy the main tenets of the poem.

(e)

THE HEROIC CONVENTION

The principles hitherto discussed went beyond the Restoration period, but there is another that applies to it alone. The gigantic proportions to which Dryden inflates Anne Killigrew is one of many examples of the gigantic inflation of human nature common at the time. In the Heroic Plays the characters are all excessive and the sentiments extreme. Lovers are violently amorous, young soldiers excessively audacious, duty pitilessly exacting and certain to conflict with the claims of love. In *Annus Mirabilis* the English naval commanders show a more than human stature and courage:

> *Our dreaded admiral from far they threat,*
> *Whose batter'd rigging their whole war receives;*
> *All bare, like some old oak which tempests beat,*
> *He stands, and sees below his scatter'd leaves.*
>
> *Heroes of old, when wounded, shelter sought;*
> *But he, who meets all danger with disdain,*
> *Ev'n in their face his ship to anchor brought*
> *And steeple-high stood propt upon the main.*
>
> *At this excess of courage all amaz'd,*
> *The foremost of his foes a while withdraw;*
> *With such respect in enter'd Rome they gaz'd*
> *Who on high chairs the godlike fathers saw.*

In the *Conquest of Granada* Almanzor is a character excessive in courage contempt of death and power of command. The comment on him after the first episode of the play is

> *How much of virtue lies in one great soul,*
> *Whose single force can multitudes control.*

Near the end of his life in the story of Sigismonda and Guiscardo, included in the *Fables*, Dryden gave his finest picture of heroic characters, a picture so convincing that we forget the convention to which they belong. These are Tancred, Duke of Salerno, and his daughter Sigismonda. Tancred discovers his daughter's secret marriage with a man of lower rank, Guiscardo, and in the ensuing quarrel between father and daughter neither will yield in the least to the other. They are towering uncompromising characters: the father wilful and tyrannical, the daughter calculatingly passionate and entirely certain of herself. We are reminded less of Dryden's earlier heroic characters than of York and Queen Margaret in the third part of Shakespeare's *Henry VI*. A second magnificent transformation of the heroic principle is in Congreve's *Way of the World*, where Mirabel and Millamant are great characters, sharply distinguished from the smaller folk that surround them. And in nothing does Congreve show greater art than in masking this sharp distinction during the actual experience of the play. As we watch, Mirabel and Millamant are two of a number of comic characters; it is only on later reflection that we recall their heroic proportions.

Sigismonda and Guiscardo and the *Way of the World* are exceptional. What we are now considering is a habit of mind so wide-spread at this time that it must mean something. Part of the meaning is the belief in decorum, mentioned above. Appearances were at the time unusually important. Even if the reality behind the appearance is defective, the appearance is better than nothing and must be maintained. Hence convention agreed to portray commanders as coming up to an ideal and superhuman standard of audacity. But decorum does not account for a thrasonical tone peculiar to the Restoration heroes. There had been heroes of other ages, whose deeds were as exaggerated as any Almanzor's; and it is instructive to compare them in other respects. Malory's Launcelot is excessive in knightly prowess but he is anything but a boastful self-sufficient man. When in a specific test he had proved himself the greatest knight in the world, he "wept as he had been a child that had been beaten". Compare this with Almanzor's protest:

But know that I alone am king of me.

The Elizabethans had their boasters and their arrogantly self-sufficient men, Tamburlaine and Bussy, but though they were attracted they condemned them. Christian humility, not stoical self-sufficiency, was still believed in. But the narrower humanism of Dryden's day and the Baconian arrogance of the new science inflated the human pretensions; and to these the practice of the heroic convention was partly due. But the peculiar thrasonical tone of this convention arose, I conjecture, not from a belief in this more exclusive humanism but in the doubts that beset it. Was man really up to these pretensions? Did the English political record really correspond to the sublime characters given to the royal rulers? Yet these pretensions were persisted in, and the very stridency of tone in which they were made expressed the uneasy conscience that lay behind them. The next century asked the same questions and gave a different answer. Pope has a very different version of human nature and he can be bitterly satirical on the qualities and exploits of an English king. And, as a whole, the eighteenth century, while believing in the unaided human reason, was modest in its claims for humanity.

Luckily Dryden's *Ode on Anne Killigrew* escapes the offensiveness of some heroic writing. Dryden's claims for his heroine are so patently ridiculous that we do not take them seriously, and they are conventionally extravagant rather than thrasonical. They thus turn our minds to those general matters of faith in which Dryden sincerely believed and of whose value no reasonable person can have any doubt: to the faith in the value of good manners and of an ordered way of life.

COLERIDGE

The Rime of the Ancient Mariner 1798

I

SO far, questions of interpretation have not been very important and they consisted partly in making obvious corrections of certain errors. Thus I could be dogmatic in repudiating the false but common notion of *Orchestra* being no more than an unorganised and irresponsible piece of fantasy. No one could reasonably doubt that Dryden did not mean his extravagant praise of Anne Killigrew to be taken at its face value: there was no need to argue the point. I went to greater length over the theological and ethical content of the *Testament of Cresseid* because this had not been perceived and a certain amount of detail was needed to carry conviction. But the *Ancient Mariner* is very different, for here certainty is much harder to attain and there is a wide possibility of varying interpretations. Where people agree is in thinking it an admirable poem—of whatever kind. To praise it, as I praised Dryden's *Ode*, is superfluous. Instead I had better give my interpretation. Only when this has been done shall I be in a position to say in what way the poem represents its age.

And first let me explain that I shall not try to criticise the poem in the sense of conveying something of the total effect. It is a rich and complicated poem, and to put in words the total effect issuing from this complication would be at once surpassingly difficult and unnecessary for the humbler objects I have in view. All I seek to do is to enumerate some of the layers of significance that go to make up the whole.

First, it is an exciting story, imitated from the old ballads, drawing much of its material from old books of

The Witches in 'Macbeth' by Fuseli

travel, enlivened by touches of realistic natural description, yet partly appealing to that side of our natures that delights in superstitions and in the supernatural. Secondly, in spite of the supernatural happenings, of which no rational explanation is given, the main events of the story happen logically in a sequence of cause and effect. In such a sequence the moral motive naturally enters, and the question arises of what this amounts to. Late in his life Coleridge censured the presence of a motivating morality. In reply to an objection of Mrs Barbauld that the poem lacked a moral he answered that it had too much:

> It ought to have had no more moral than the Arabian Nights' tale of the merchant's sitting down to eat dates by the side of a well, and throwing the shells aside, and lo! a genie starts up, and says he *must* kill the aforesaid merchant, *because* one of the date shells had, it seems, put out the eye of the genie's son.[1]

Probably Coleridge was stung to perversity by Mrs Barbauld's being so stupid, and did not mean what he said. In truth, the moral story, the punishment of a crime, is the core of the poem; each part ends with a reference to the crime, the killing of the albatross: remove the moral, and the poem collapses. Granted the moral, we must beware of narrowing it to the familiar modern doctrine of kindness to animals. If the albatross had been a crow or vulture or other bird of ill omen, there would have been no crime in shooting it; yet by humanitarian standards the act would have been just as bad. The reasons for not shooting the albatross were superstitious or at least primitive. By standards of superstition animals are good or bad. It is unlucky to kill the good; the bad (the toad, for instance) can be persecuted to any extent. The albatross was a good bird, and they "hailed it in God's name". It was also their guest, and in a primitive world treachery to a guest was a terrible crime. Coleridge's gloss sums the matter up: "The ancient Mariner inhospitably killeth the

[1] *Table Talk* for 31 May 1830.

pious bird of good omen." Whether the act itself apart from its consequences can be motivated is a matter of opinion. Should we simply accept it as a piece of plot-mechanism, like Lear's resolution to divide his kingdom, or should we detect a reason? Certainly there is a very simple reason to hand. The act could be interpreted as the essential act of devilment, the act of pride, of the un-bridled assertion of the self. It was what Satan did when he rebelled and what Defoe made Crusoe do when he thrice rejected God's offer of a virtuous middle way of life. Whatever the answer, we are suitably impressed by the enormity of the mariner's crime and readily accept the straits into which he falls. The way he gets out of these straits is also motivated but with a richness that makes it difficult not to encroach here on other layers of the poem's meaning. One reason for his escape is the sheer fulfilment of a frightful penance: he issues out of his prison like a prisoner who has served his time, whether repentant or not. And this punitive motive corresponds well enough to the purely superstitious crime of killing a bird of good omen. But there is the further reason of his blessing the water-snakes. And this was an act of repentance, a moral reversal of his grossly self-regarding act of killing the albatross, a forgetfulness of self in recognising the beauty of something quite independent. The crime, however, is not expiated at once. One of the two voices in the air says there is more penance to do. It is the one defect in the poem's structure that this further penance hardly exists and that the final expiation in line 442 ("And now this spell was snapt...") comes in very casually. Having learnt to expect motivation, we are disappointed when it is lacking. Even if we assume that the penance is now really complete, we still miss a further act of repentance to corre-spond to the blessing of the water-snakes. Thenceforward everything is credible in its context. The crime has been such that we accept the mariner's final doom of having periodically to relive his old experience through recount-ing his tale.

I have spoken of the simple narrative interest and of the moral motivation together because the second helps the first along: a logical is more emphatic than a mere casual sequence. As Lowes says in his *Road to Xanadu*[1]: "The sequence which follows the Mariner's initial act accomplishes two ends: it unifies and it 'credibilizes' the poem". But Lowes notices something more about the morality: its truth to the ordinary experience of life. He writes [2]:

> The train of cause and consequence is more than a consolidating factor of the poem. It happens to be life, as every human being knows it. You do a foolish or an evil deed, and its results come home to you. And they are apt to fall on others too. You repent, and a load is lifted from your soul. But you have not thereby escaped your deed. You attain forgiveness, but cause and effect work on unmoved, and life to the end may be the continued reaping of the repented deed's results.

Though this is not how we think of the poem when we read it, we do ratify Lowes's words on reflection. And they are important, for they convey a part of the meaning that is too often forgotten. And it is precisely the blend of this sheer truth to human experience with the narrative power the fantastic happenings and the brilliant pictures that makes the *Ancient Mariner* so rich and so surprising.

But the *Ancient Mariner* is more than a fascinating story with a moral. It may be that H. I'A. Fausset is right in seeing it as an allegory of Coleridge's own life: his strange mind, his terrors, his loquacity. The Mariner, repeating his tale, may well be Coleridge, "seeking relief throughout his life in endless monologues". But even if Fausset is right, he is indicating a very minor layer of the poem's meaning. What matters is not that Coleridge should be speaking for himself but that he should be speaking for many others. Miss Bodkin in her *Archetypal Patterns in Poetry* chooses the *Ancient Mariner* as one of the poems

[1] P. 299. [2] P. 298.

"the ground of whose appeal is most evidently the impression of the inner life", but she rightly does not confine the inner life to Coleridge's. And if, as I think we should, we take the Mariner's voyage as a mental one, it should figure the adventures not of Coleridge alone but of all mental voyagers.

Once we postulate an allegory we are beset with dangers, above all with the temptation to grow excited, to see too much, to mistake a simple picturesque detail for a complicated moral truth. I will try to keep to the more obvious and plausible significances.

The general drift of the poem in its mental action can readily be recognised by two passages from other poets: Webster,

> *My soul like to a ship in a black storm*
> *Is driven I know not whither;*

and Shelley,

> *The breath whose might I have invoked in song*
> *Descends on me; my spirit's bark is driven*
> *Far from the shore, far from the trembling throng*
> *Whose sails were never to the tempest given;*
> *The massy earth and sphered skies are riven.*
> *I am borne darkly, fearfully, afar!*

The sea-voyage, then, indicates spiritual *adventure*, as the ordinary journey or pilgrimage indicates the course of normal life. And it is not everyone who goes out of his way to seek adventure. There is a passage in Coleridge's prose[1] that both says this and has its bearing on the *Ancient Mariner*.

The first range of hills, that encircles the scanty vale of human life, is the horizon for the majority of its inhabitants. On *its* ridges the common sun is born and departs. From *them* the stars rise, and touching *them* they vanish. By the many, even this range, the natural limit and bulwark of the vale, is but imperfectly known. Its higher ascents are too often hidden by mists

[1] *Biographia Literaria*, xii.

and clouds from uncultivated swamps, which few have courage or curiosity to penetrate. To the multitude below these vapours appear, now as the dark haunts of terrific agents, on which none may intrude with impunity; and now all aglow, with colours not their own, they are gazed at as the splendid palaces of happiness and power. But in all ages there have been a few, who measuring and sounding the rivers of the vale at the feet of their furthest inaccessible falls have learned, that the sources must be far higher and far inward; a few, who even in the level streams have detected elements, which neither the vale itself nor the surrounding mountains contained or could supply. . . . It is the essential mark of the true philosopher to rest satisfied with no imperfect light, as long as the impossibility of attaining a fuller knowledge has not been demonstrated.

The Ancient Mariner and his ship represent the small but persisting class of mental adventurers who are not content with the appearances surrounding them but who attempt to get behind. (It may be added that though the class is small it stands for a universal impulse which is dormant in most minds and not absent from them.) Further, and here I recognise the danger of seeing too much, it is possible that the different degrees of nearness to normality represented in the poem do correspond to the apprehension of such degrees in actual life. The harbour-town, occurring in a narrative, is less real than the wedding-guest and the wedding but more so than the realms visited in the voyage; and these degrees of reality can hardly be without their effect.

Granted that the Mariner and his voyage signify the mental adventure of an unusually inquiring spirit, the outline of that adventure becomes tolerably clear, while it would be senseless to seek more than an outline. From the social point of view these spiritual adventurers are criminals: they disturb the existing order and they imply a criticism of the accepted round of life: they are self-appointed outcasts. The shooting of the albatross in the present context was an anti-social act: something that by everyday rules would not be done. And the avenging spirit takes the Mariner into a region and a situation the utter loneliness of which is both the logical consequence and the avengement of his revolt against society. This same region is one more version of that aridity that besets all isolated mental voyagers at one stage of their voyage. Other versions are Donne's conceit of himself in *A Nocturnal upon St Lucy's Day* as the quintessence of the primeval nothingness out of which God created the world; the emptiness experienced by the poet in Shelley's *Alastor*, who, when he awakes from his dreams, sees the "garish hills" and "vacant woods", while his "wan eyes"

> *Gaze on the empty scene as vacantly*
> *As ocean's moon looks on the moon in heaven;*

and the landscape in Browning's *Childe Roland*. The Mariner escapes from his isolation by the enlargement of his sympathies in the manner least expected and he is allowed to return to common life. And he does so as a changed man. He has repented of his isolation; his greatest satisfaction is to worship in company with his fellows of all ages. But he is still the marked man, the outcast, the Wandering Jew, the victim of his own thoughts. Further, although he has been judged by society, he has the reward of the courage that propels the mental adventurer: that of arresting and disturbing and teaching those who have had no such experiences. And this ambivalent criterion enriches the poem incalculably.

But there may be yet one more important layer of meaning; something so simple and fundamental that it extends beyond the rarer sphere of self-imposed mental adventure to the common inevitable workings of the human mind. Miss Bodkin sees in the *Ancient Mariner* a rendering of the pattern of rebirth,[1] which is at once the theme of tragedy and a very law of human life: the process of renovation through destruction. This theme is certainly present. It was only through the destruction of his old state of

[1] *Archetypal Patterns in Poetry*, chap. II.

mind that the Mariner was able to achieve the new, enlarged state of mind that could include the water-snakes in its sympathies. But the *Ancient Mariner* is unlike the most satisfying works that render the theme, for instance the *Oresteia* or *Lycidas*, in that the renovation brought about is less powerful than the thing from whose destruction it has sprung. There is nothing to correspond to the thrust of energy that ends *Lycidas* with

> *To-morrow to fresh woods, and pastures new.*

The Ancient Mariner has been born again into a ghostly existence, not rejuvenated. And the haunting terror of the destructive experience remains the dominant theme of the poem:

> *O Wedding-Guest! this soul hath been*
> *Alone on a wide wide sea.*

So much for some of the layers of meaning. It is (may I repeat?) their co-existence and their interplay that makes the *Ancient Mariner* a poem of which one never tires. Finally, and before I go on to the ideas which Coleridge shared with his age, there is a detail in the plotting which parallels the co-existence of two layers of meaning. At one of the high points of the poem there is a discrepancy between the emotional-rhythmical plot and the asserted or factual plot. I refer to lines 257 onwards. The stanza beginning with 257 is the climax of the Mariner's suffering, and the bare factual meaning of the words that follow is that the suffering continues.

> *Her beams bemocked the sultry main,*
> *Like April hoar-frost spread;*
> *But where the ship's huge shadow lay,*
> *The charméd water burnt alway*
> *A still and awful red.*

The moonbeams are *hostile*, mocking the sultry main, while the water beneath the ship's shadow was a *horrible* red. It is only later that the mood changes and the Mariner blesses the water-snakes. But rhythmically and emotionally the change had already come in line 263 with

> *The moving Moon went up the sky*
> *And no where did abide:*
> *Softly she was going up,*
> *And a star or two beside.*

The relaxation in the rhythm is unmistakeable, and the playing off this relaxation against the contradictory assertion that the horror is still there is a wonderful poetic stroke. And this playing off is confirmed by line 287 when we learn that the Mariner blessed the water-snakes *unaware*. The rhythm of line 263 is the index of the first unconscious motion of the mind towards renewal.

II

The claims made above for a complexity of meaning in the *Ancient Mariner* have a direct bearing on the extent to which the poem reflects the contemporary world. Most people think of it as a delightful poem and typical of its age principally for arousing our sense of wonder. Fewer will think of it as exhibiting many contemporary habits of thought. Yet it exhibits them so richly and in some points contrasts so aptly with the other poems I have chosen that it embarrasses by the amount of material it offers. All I can do is to select some of the main topics.

(a)

RELIGIOUS FEELING

A very remarkable thing in the *Ancient Mariner* is the strength of the religious or at least numinous feeling. And equally remarkable is the great variety of such feeling it contains. In these matters it speaks for a part of its age. Indeed but a part; for after the Augustan Age it becomes increasingly hard to find ways of thought and feeling uni-

versally accepted in England. And along with an un-
doubted expansion of religious sensibility was the steady
advance of the utilitarian and scientific principles.

To begin with more general matters the *Ancient Mariner* is permeated with the sense of what people now call
the numinous, with the sense of impalpable spirituality.
It haunts the borders of the unknown and gives hints of
terrors and joys that are awaiting exploration. It is true
that Coleridge's knowledge of medieval angelology and
demonology gives his poem a semblance of preciseness,
but in addition there is this pervading sense of the numinous, which unites it to some of the early Wordsworth, to
much of Shelley, to Ruskin and much nineteenth century
writing, and which separates it from any of the poems
hitherto discussed. This side of the *Ancient Mariner* may
be vaguely religious but it is untheological. The *Testament
of Cresseid* is not primarily a religious poem, but its tragic
story is conducted under a precise, though general, theology. What theology there is is schematic. Henryson is
more certain and mathematically correct about his planetary powers than Coleridge is about his spirits. If Henryson
had used these spirits, he would have sorted graded and
labelled them. Coleridge was learned in medieval theology
and he knows about the chain of being. But he uses the
links in it out of their old context and in a new context of
vague numinous evocation. The spirits in the *Ancient
Mariner* are akin to Shelley's:

> *Oh! there are spirits of the air*
> *And genii of the evening breeze,*
> *And gentle ghosts—*

and alien to the precisely ordered spiritual hierarchies of
Dionysius the Areopagite. And the albatross is no part of
a scheme but a detached symbol, useful to the poet in
isolation.

Along with the numinous is the hint of pantheism,
again uniting Coleridge with Wordsworth and Tennyson
and later writers. This hint is given by the episode of

blessing the water-snakes. The Mariner watches them not as a past age would have done as moral emblems or as servants of man, or as witnesses of the ingenuity of God's craftsmanship, but as creatures with a life of their own. In so doing he is eminently modern; for apart from a purely scientific interest this delight in the autonomy of animals, in their having their own proper business, is to-day the chief attraction of watching them. Such a feeling need not lead to pantheism, witness Hopkins's very orthodox poem, the *Windhover*, where with the words, "my heart in hiding stirred for a bird", the feeling comes in. It was the bird's going about its business utterly separate from and oblivious of the watcher that gave the special excitement. Nevertheless it is easy to see how such a feeling can tend to pantheism. Once you give animals a life of their own, you can easily suggest that it is just as good a life as the human. And once you do that, you tend to confound the classic divisions of existence and to make no unclosable chasm between inanimate and animate, between spiritual and non-spiritual. And with these divisions gone, it is natural to identify God and creation and to make him both all phenomena and its animating spirit,

> *one intellectual breeze*
> *At once the Soul of each, and God of all,*[1]

rather than a person who has created his separate world out of nothing.

Next (and very obviously) there is the superstitious side appealing to that in human nature which dreads giving offence to a little-known and unpredictable supernatural power. In exploiting this feeling Coleridge was at one with his age. The eighteenth century as a whole had tended both to overestimate the speed with which such feelings were dwindling in the human mind and to dislike their occurrence in earlier ages. In compensation the next age paid them marked attention. The superstitions attached to the albatross have been mentioned already. The

---

[1] Coleridge, *The Eolian Harp*, 47-8.

wedding-guest's fear of the Ancient Mariner is superstitious: he might have the evil as well as the compelling eye. And the Mariner himself, although self-propelled from land to land, is yet akin to the outcasts whose gift of bringing ill-luck to whatever land they inhabit makes them wanderers over the earth. Most obviously of all, the ballad form of the poem unites it with the medieval ballad and the world of the Fairy Tale. It thus represents a contemporary happening. People were tiring of the restricted anthology of Fairy Tales—mainly the selections and adaptations of Perrault—that prevailed in polite eighteenth century circles. The brothers Grimm were collecting their folklore during the Romantic period and in 1812 began to publish their *Kinder- und Hausmärchen* (first translated into English in 1823). Nor can the crudest of all contemporary exploitations of the feeling for superstition be left unmentioned, the Gothic novel, for however remote in subtlety from the *Ancient Mariner* it does present some community of substance.

The Gothic novel suggests still another side of religion, the antiquarian; for the *Ancient Mariner* is very much of an antiquarian, Neo-Gothic poem. It is so good that we tend to forget this, just as much Neo-Gothic architecture is bad enough to remind us constantly that it is pastiche. Along with the ballad form is the medieval Catholic setting. The setting is a world of mariolatry, hermits, shriving, guardian saints and angels. However different the effect, this antiquarianism is comparable with Scott's and it has its contemporary importance. George Borrow blamed Scott for the Oxford Movement; and though he may have erred in concentrating his blame on one man, there is no doubt that the very wide antiquarian interest of the early nineteenth century in medieval things prepared the ground for a large religious movement that went right beyond the antiquarian. The hearty fun of the *Ingoldsby Legends* at the expense of the Middle Ages has its relation to the *Ancient Mariner* and testifies to the interests which contributed to the Oxford Movement.

And lastly the *Ancient Mariner* is religious in a much profounder way. Like the *Testament of Cresseid* it deals not only with the dreadful experience but with the salvation of a human soul. The Mariner is a sinner, and his blessing of the water-snakes is not only a reversal of feeling but an act of repentance. Again, the religion is little schematised. Cresseid, we can clearly infer, committed two of the Seven Deadly Sins, and her repentance followed a dictated plan. If the Mariner's sin was pride, we say so only by conjecture, and his conversion and repentance are conducted not on a plan but on the suppositions of human psychology. An interesting comparison is with T. S. Eliot's *Family Reunion*, suggesting that Coleridge looks forward not back. The turning point in Harry's mind is when he decides to follow the Eumenides not to fly from them. Just so the Mariner blesses the water-snakes instead of abhorring them. Again Coleridge speaks for his age. Between him and Dryden had interposed the expansion of the old Puritanism into the Wesleyan movement with a resultant emphasis on a sense of personal sin and on conversion. But to follow up this topic would anticipate my section on individualism.

With such different religious strains present simultaneously in a poem of six hundred lines it is astonishing that we experience no discomfort or sense of incongruity in the reading. On the contrary it is only with an effort that we can distinguish and perceive separately these strains; and we are surprised to find they are so many. Coleridge had every right to call the imagination the esemplastic power after having given so perfect a demonstration of its unifying operation.

(b)

NATURE

Not only in religion but in nature Coleridge sees different things. Natural objects have ceased to be clearly arranged in the chain of being, but they can be numinous or terrifyingly fantastic, or purely picturesque, or correlatives of human emotion. The variety is astonishing, as the quality of descriptive power is superlatively good. For simple picturesque effect no contemporary or later poet has surpassed the description of the moonlit harbour on the return:

> *The harbour-bay was clear as glass,*
> *So smoothly it was strewn!*
> *And on the bay the moonlight lay,*
> *And the shadow of the Moon.*

> *The rock shone bright, the kirk no less,*
> *That stands above the rock:*
> *The moonlight steeped in silentness*
> *The steady weathercock.*

But the terms in which one of the Voices describes another moonlit seascape are very different indeed.

> *Still as a slave before his lord,*
> *The ocean hath no blast;*
> *His great bright eye most silently*
> *Up to the Moon is cast—*

> *If he may know which way to go;*
> *For she guides him smooth or grim.*
> *See, brother, see! how graciously*
> *She looketh down on him!*

There is little of the purely picturesque here but much that stirs our hidden and vaguely defined emotions. This utter servitude of the sea, more familiarly a symbol of unregulated violence or, considered in its vastness, of eternity, comes as a shock, and yet, with that portion of our mind that can still understand animism and magical habits of thought, we respond. It is interesting to compare Davies's lines on the same theme containing the same metaphor:

> *For lo, the sea, that fleets about the land*
> *And like a girdle clips her solid waist,*

Music and measure both doth understand;
For his great crystal eye is always cast
Up to the moon and on her fixed fast;
And as she danceth in her pallid sphere,
So danceth he about the centre here.

There is nothing primitive in Davies's thought, but with fantastic and sophisticated ornament he decks out a fixed inherited piece of information. For the emotional use of nature, the simple "pathetic fallacy", take another lunar description:

Her beams bemocked the sultry main,

or the single epithet of "*star-dogged* Moon".

The uses to which the nineteenth century put nature are well enough known to make it unnecessary to say more than that in his various modes of description Coleridge was the representative of his age.

(c)

ABSENCE OF POLITICS

There is a total lack of politics in the *Ancient Mariner*. Admittedly with such a subject politics are not to be looked for; yet here is a poem of six hundred lines and without the glimmering of a reference to any body politic. It was not that Coleridge was not interested in politics: on the contrary he had just written some very political poetry. In both these matters he represents his age. There was much political activity and yet how little do politics get into the best literature. Cowper's most poignant and effective verse is personal not political. Crabbe is social rather than political. Blake, according to Bronowski, is full of covert politics, but he is read for other things. Wordsworth was passionately interested in politics and spent much time in thinking on them and some time in writing on them in prose. Yet his effective verse, when it concerns man, concerns individual and unpolitical man. Shelley indeed is political, but it is not his political verse we most know him by. Keats is not political at all. This poetical shift away from politics is new. In Henryson politics and the Church were so interconnected that his orthodox theology can include the political field, not to speak of his serene acceptance of the social divisions of the Commonwealth. In *Orchestra* Elizabeth and her court have their inalienable importance in the world scheme, just as the idea of royalty and the history plays form an organic part of the complete works of Shakespeare. Even if for Shakespeare the individual may count ultimately for most, there is, even in his most purely tragic or romantic plays, a wonderfully strong counterpoise to these other motives in the powerful political values in the background. In the *Ode on Anne Killigrew* the royalism is organic. But in the most intense and serious poetry of the Romantics (Byron perhaps excepted) the body politic and organised man have dwindled in importance, while individual man with all the complexities and perplexities of his cerebration counts for so much more: a statement which leads to the next topic.

(d)

INDIVIDUALISM

The *Ancient Mariner* speaks for its age in turning from social man to individual man and in caring for his inner motivation more than for his external activities. The two trends are not the same but they spring from such similar causes that it is hard to keep them apart.

For the novelty of this individualism contrast the *Ancient Mariner* with what Dryden makes of Anne Killigrew. Dryden praises her accomplishments with an extravagance which, taken at its face value, is ridiculous. But it is so ridiculous that we cannot possibly apply what he says, to one person. Inevitably our minds turn from the individual to the class of poets and thence to general ideas

F

about poetry and painting; they come to rest on the social and on the political. Coleridge in his way is not less extravagant than Dryden, but with how different a result. *His* extravagances do correspond to what can take place in a human brain; they spring not from decorum but from a kind of truth. Even if they make a fascinating objective narrative, they do, in suggesting a psychological or even pathological reality, direct our attention to, or rather into, the individual mind.

The *Ancient Mariner* indeed illustrates wonderfully the psychological trend of thought which, beginning with Locke, grew powerful in the early nineteenth century, and has been a dominant thing in men's lives till the present day. Whether the death of Freud marks its decline remains for a later age to perceive.

Coleridge has put his psychology in terms of the religious idea of salvation, of sin and forgiveness. It happens that Henryson dealt with the same topic; and it is instructive to compare or contrast the two poets on this point. Cresseid, however pathetic a figure, behaves according to a formulated, classic set of rules. She falls into two classic sins; she is punished condignly; she repents; she is assured of salvation. The result is that even though her story is extremely moving it does not individualise the sufferer, rather it turns her into a version of the medieval Everyman. The Mariner, on the other hand, although given a greater semblance of acting by rules than most Romantic figures, behaves primarily according to the inner motions of the human heart. He blesses the water-snakes unaware; and how remote this *unaware* from the mathematical precision of medieval motivation. Again, the Mariner takes a journey; yet how different that journey from the pilgrimage governed by the precise moral geography of the medieval allegory. Between the medieval reliance on a religion whose rules were precisely laid down and the Mariner's heart-searching interposes a large change of ways of thought. Protestantism had put the weight on the individual act of faith as against the sufficient performance of duties. Puritanism by agonising over the act of faith had opened up strange byways in the human mind. And in the eighteenth century the scientific curiosity of Locke about the human brain and the spread of Puritan habits of thought through the Wesleys combined to effect a revolution. Not to speak of the self-communings of Rousseau. Bunyan's *Pilgrim's Progress* is a wonderfully apt work of transition. In form it is highly schematised and follows the old tradition of the medieval allegory; but in effect it expresses the Puritan exaltation of faith over works, and shadows not the keeping of a set of rules or the fulfilment of certain obligations but the inner struggle to be saved.

In finding that the *Ancient Mariner* typifies Romantic individualism I have brought up a very obvious and familiar topic: more so than any mentioned hitherto, through its being so close to us. But it is precisely the familiar things with which I am principally concerned, and though this additional familiarity suggests brevity it must not be allowed to impose silence. I will mention at least two sides of Romantic individualism, both implied by the *Ancient Mariner*.

First, with the stress on the individual mind, it was natural that the less obvious as well as the more obvious parts of the mind should be taken into account. When a man agonises over a decision and relies on his own natural powers of choice and not on a set of religious ordinances or social conventions he will find that he makes his decision for reasons he cannot fathom or analyse. As the Mariner blessed the water-snakes unaware, so he makes his decisions not by conscious weighing in a balance but intuitively. Along with the new preciseness and rigorous discipline of the scientific movement of the nineteenth century was a shift of emphasis from the conscious to the unconscious part of the mind, from the sophisticated to the primitive, from reasoned choices to intuition. It was a shift carried to extremes in D. H. Lawrence, for instance, for whom "politics, principles, right and wrong" are a "desert void" and who pronounces that "when it comes to living, we live through our instincts and our intuitions". Further illustration is superfluous.

Second, when choices are to be made not by a preordained set of rules but by individual preference, it becomes natural that such a choice should be more highly valued if it is new and surprising than if it is repetitive; for repetition might easily become a formula and a fixed criterion. Hence, in part, the nineteenth century cult of originality.[1] How powerful this cult is we can see at once by the instinctive welcome we give the word. A headmaster, considering the testimonial of a would-be assistant, little as he would like a man to be odd, would emit approval if he read that the man had a vein of originality. Contrariwise to say of someone that he has no originality is an unmitigatedly adverse criticism. Such a state of affairs did not exist before the nineteenth century.

Thirdly, Romantic individualism with its interest in the composition of the human mind shows itself in the trend of literary criticism in the nineteenth century. From Wordsworth with his talk of the passions to Bradley with his analysis of motives, criticism has been predominantly psychological. Poetry for Sidney was the glimpse of a state of things better than the actualities of life after the Fall of man allow, for Rymer an exhibition of decorum; for Wordsworth and the nineteenth century it is a rendering of individual human emotion.

Lastly, the Ancient Mariner represents a form of individualism characteristic of the Romantic period rather than of the rest of the nineteenth century. In their love of the individual the Romantics had a special fondness for a type so differentiated and original that he could not fit into ordinary human society. This type was so sensitive, or so wicked, and so obsessed by his own thoughts that he could

---

[1] *Originality* is an ambiguous word. Its cult includes the idea of scientific discovery. We speak of "original research", meaning fresh discovery but not necessarily by means of an unusual or original exercise of mind.

not stay still but was driven on an unending pilgrimage. He forms a part of the true mythology of the Romantic age, and the Ancient Mariner is an eminent example of him. Shelley's Alastor is another example, and his self-description in *Adonais* perhaps the classic account of the type.

> *Midst others of less note, came one frail Form,*
> *A phantom among men; companionless*
> *As the last cloud of an expiring storm*
> *Whose thunder is its knell; he, as I guess,*
> *Had gazed on Nature's naked loveliness,*
> *Actaeon-like, and now he fled astray*
> *With feeble steps o'er the world's wilderness,*
> *And his own thoughts, along that rugged way,*
> *Pursued, like raging hounds, their father and their prey.*

The Byronic hero, though more of a man of action than Shelley's poet in *Alastor*, is clearly one of the type. Marmaduke, in Wordsworth's *Borderers*, turns at the end into the outcast and wanderer, unfit for human society:

> *A wanderer must I go . . .*
> *No human ear shall ever hear me speak;*
> *No human dwelling ever give me food,*
> *Or sleep, or rest: but over waste and wild,*
> *In search of nothing that this earth can give,*
> *But expiation, will I wander on.*

At his worst the self-propelled wanderer expressed a kind of snobbery of pessimism: only the inferior and insensitive find repose; the best people are like Io, driven round the world by the gadfly of remorse or of hypertrophied sensibilities. But Coleridge is exempt from the accusation of any such snobbery. Whatever his weaknesses his self-pity or the sanctimoniousness of his repentances, his desire to explore strange and frightening mental regions was genuine, as were his courage and persistence in maintaining the quest.

(*e*)

COMPLEXITY

I spoke above of the diversity of the *Ancient Mariner*, of the multiple layers of meaning, of the different uses to which nature is put. This diversity is the true index of the vast complication of life that occurred in the Romantic period. It was as if the data for living had suddenly been multiplied. Not only were people learning more about the human mind but about human history and about the physical world. The industrial revolution was yet another complication. The situation was all the more difficult because on the whole the eighteenth century had pretended that their own rather simpler world was much simpler than it actually was. There is no need to labour the predicament of the Romantics, for we have inherited it and many added burdens of knowledge. The *Ancient Mariner* is modern in quite a special way through expressing, however subtly, this terrifying complexity.

It was an irony that the urge to put the burden of choice on the individual should have occurred when the difficulties of choosing had been incalculably increased.

Automedon with the Horses of Achilles by Regnault

SWINBURNE

Hertha 1870

I

I KNOW no Victorian poem of comparable length that catches up so much contemporary and anticipates so much modern thought. One reason is that Swinburne thinks in European rather than in English terms and in so doing is prophetic of the decision England, much against her will, has been forced to make: that of acknowledging herself as for ever a part of Europe. Browning may go to live in Italy, Tennyson may deprecate the violence of the 1848 revolutions on the Continent and foretell the federation of the world, but in themselves they are much more English than Swinburne, who is really open to foreign trends of thought and is the herald of our now increased internationalism.

Hertha is a difficult poem, and I doubt whether most readers have perceived the wealth of meaning it contains. Since I have seen no exposition, I had better spend some time in explaining the allusions, or as many as I have understood. It is interesting that of the five poems chosen the most recent should be far the most difficult to decipher.

Songs before Sunrise, to which *Hertha* belongs, were written between 1867 and 1870 at the instigation of the Italian patriot and republican, Mazzini, whom Swinburne knew personally and admired enthusiastically. Italy was in process of union through the advancement of Victor Emmanuel and the house of Piedmont. But Mazzini was firmly anti-royalist and hoped for a revolution at Rome (then part of the Vatican State) which would liberate and finally unite Italy, overthrowing the house of Piedmont and establishing a republic. His hopes were ill-grounded; nevertheless he succeeded in animating Swinburne with his zeal for an Italian republic. Then, in 1869, when Swinburne had written many of *Songs before Sunrise*, Pope Pius IX summoned the Oecumenical Council which asserted the doctrine of papal infallibility and adopted the "Syllabus" condemning the liberal doctrines of the age. It was Swinburne's fury against this Council that called forth three of the most vigorous poems in *Songs before Sunrise*: *Tiresias*, the *Hymn of Man*, and *Hertha*. This fury explains why in *Hertha* Swinburne is so pointedly explicitly and defiantly heterodox. Another topical reference is the line

> *Green leaves of thy labour, white flowers of thy thought, and red fruit of thy death,*

where the colours indicate the flag of united Italy. But though elicited by actual events *Hertha* propounds a very general philosophy of man's destiny and in so doing voices certain large general sentiments of its age.

Although events in Italy and an Italian patriot inspired Swinburne to write *Hertha*, he chose his setting from Teutonic mythology. Hertha, who is imagined to address the poem to mankind, is the Teutonic goddess of earth, standing for what might be popularly called the "Life Force"; while the "tree many-rooted" is Yggdrasil, the Teutonic world-tree. Yggdrasil represents all nature, the power holding heaven earth and hell together. At its foot is Niflheim or hell, a region of darkness, where a dragon gnaws at the roots. Above is an eagle; and a squirrel runs between dragon and eagle inciting them to battle. Swinburne also uses the Teutonic myth of the twilight of the gods in stanza thirty-seven:

> *For his twilight is come on him,*
> *His anguish is here;*
> *And his spirits gaze dumb on him,*
> *Grown grey from his fear;*
> *And his hour taketh hold on him stricken, the last of his*
> *infinite year.*

For doctrine Swinburne borrowed elements from oriental

pantheism and from the nineteenth century religion of humanity popularised by Comte, but, as will be seen, his Teutonic setting has a strong doctrinal bearing also, though Swinburne may have been scarcely aware of it.

I will now explain some of the significance of *Hertha* and how it evolves. In general it must be remembered that *Hertha* belongs to *Songs before Sunrise* and that the symbolism of the heavens is based on the idea of sunrise. The sun is not one of the smaller units of the galaxy but the supreme luminary that quenches the feeble tapers of the stars. Similarly the stars are not (as in the *Ode to Anne Killigrew* or *Adonais*) symbols of eternity but uncertain lights destined to extinction. Throughout the poem the goddess Hertha speaks and in the first three stanzas she says she contains all being and all processes within herself, gods as well as men. In the following exposition I refer to stanzas and lines within the stanzas. In 1. 4 *equal and whole* refer, among other things, to the conservation of energy and the indestructibility of matter. In 2. 5 *thy* refers to man; and Swinburne means that the seed of humanity was contained within the sum of things from the beginning. There was no separate act of creation, an idea taken up later. In 3. 1 *first life*=protozoa. Swinburne knows and refers to contemporary theories of evolution. In stanzas four to eight Swinburne puts the comprehensiveness of Hertha in terms of oriental pantheism. Not only did creation evolve out of Hertha and not come into being by a separate act, but there is no line of demarcation between creator and created. These are metaphysical stanzas, in ingenuity not unlike Donne though different in language. See especially the last three lines of stanza six, which say ingeniously that Hertha contains within herself, and has always contained, all the evolutionary processes of existence. In stanza seven Swinburne attacks the doctrine that man and god are separate; and in so doing he is thinking of the Oecumenical Council and the fundamental Catholic doctrine that God and man are very separate indeed, God having created him out of nothing by a special act of creation. Stanzas nine to thirteen develop the theme of how man was or was not created. We know nothing of the process of our creation. The rest of nature can give no information to that effect. And the goddess of nature, who speaks, tells us that we were not created but evolved out of the substance of all existence, out of herself. It is just possible that Swinburne here echoes the arch-blasphemy of Satan in *Paradise Lost* [1]:

> *We know no time when we were not as now;*
> *Know none before us, self-begot, self-rais'd*
> *By our own quickning power.*

Anyhow Swinburne certainly echoes the general blasphemy of which Milton's is the classic expression in English poetry. Stanzas fourteen to nineteen, which praise Hertha and attack gods and creeds, arise naturally from the last; for if creation is a myth, a creator is so too. In stanza fifteen she tells man to live not by creed but by natural instincts, which are good. But in seventeen we learn that to live naturally is not to live easily. Hertha lavished life on us: we live according to her if we lavish life in return; even to the death. Swinburne does not preach ignoble ease like Belial but the doctrine of blood and tears like Garibaldi. In stanza nineteen *the shadow called God* is the moon, the mere shadow or derivative of the sun. Hertha used the gods for her evolutionary purposes; now they are superfluous, for man can enjoy the sun. In stanza twenty Swinburne rises to his climax in describing Hertha through the image of the tree Yggdrasil:

> *The tree many-rooted*
> *That swells to the sky*
> *With frondage red-fruited,*
> *The life-tree am I;*
> *In the buds of your lives is the sap of my leaves: ye shall live*
> *and not die.*

And in stanzas twenty-one to -four he gives details of the tree, some obscure. In twenty-two the reference is to the

[1] v. 856-8.

dragon of Teutonic mythology in the darkness of the roots
below wounding the bark. But the welling vitality of the
tree heals the trivial wounds. The tree includes the stars,
the false but useful flickers destined to be quenched at
sunrise. In stanza twenty-three past ages are compared to
dead leaves at the tree's base. Stanzas twenty-five to thirty-
one are mainly historical. In twenty-six and twenty-seven
the references are to the violence of geological evolution
and of human dynastic change: this violence does not
threaten Hertha with ruin. In twenty-eight Hertha admits
that though history, the process of growth, has been
terrible, she has survived; and (an important addition)
life, mere life, is self-justified. Stanzas thirty-one -two and
-five bring us back to the present, and man is exhorted to
free himself now from false creeds. In stanzas thirty-four
-six -seven and -eight the motive of the twilight of the
gods enters: god and his angels are doomed and they know
it. In the last two stanzas we learn that Truth is the one
religion and that man is the apex of the evolutionary process.

I have chosen to speak of *Hertha's* meaning before its
poetic merit because, unlike the other four poems, it
attracts a modern initially more through its ideas than its
form. But before I go on to speak of the contemporary
ways of thinking it represents I must now ask whether it
fulfils one of the conditions of the poems chosen: that of
high literary merit. Certainly we have in *Hertha* the
curious spectacle of current ideas in a very unfashionable
poetic guise, but one day the position will be reversed.
The ideas will look old-fashioned, the poetic form will
take its place with other discarded but accepted forms,
and *Hertha* will be read first for the poetry and then for
the habits of thought.

As a poem *Hertha* is eminent for the energy of metrical
movement and the fecundity of rhyme. These together
express a fine mental exuberance and confidence. The
verse is held tightly in and compressed in the four short
rhymed lines of each stanza and then breaks out and spills
itself into the long fifth line, to be saved from mere waste

by the closing rhyme. It is easy and delightful on the muscles of speech: excellent for reading aloud and declaiming. *Hertha* is poetry that has the simple function of rousing the blood: and as such it is not to be despised. It does the kind of thing that Whitman and Browning did, and, I think, better: more thoroughly and with greater technical skill. Further, the thought is close: Swinburne gets more into the space than the other two. Nevertheless, for all its virtues, *Hertha* is the least civilised of my five poems. It is in fact a fine and highly elaborated example of what Santayana has called the Poetry of Barbarism. Of Browning and Whitman, whom he takes as examples of such poets, he wrote as follows [1]:

> Both poets represent, therefore, and are admired for representing, what may be called the poetry of barbarism in the most accurate and descriptive sense of this word. For the barbarian is the man who regards his passions as their own excuse for being; who does not domesticate them either by understanding their cause or conceiving their ideal goal. He is the man who does not know his derivations nor perceive his tendencies, but who merely feels and acts, valuing in his life its force and its filling, but being careless of its purpose and its form. His delight is in abundance and vehemence; his art, like his life, shows an exclusive respect for quantity and splendour of materials. His scorn for what is poorer and weaker than himself is only surpassed by his ignorance of what is higher.

Swinburne, with his classical erudition and his contacts with French authors, would seem at first sight to be less barbaric than Whitman or Browning. But one has only to compare his conception of liberty with that of the man he thought he was indebted to, Mazzini, to see how Swinburne could coarsen in borrowing. Santayana's account fits *Hertha* well: like his barbarian "who regards his passions as their own excuse for being", Hertha protests that mere growth is self-justified, while the barbaric regard for quantity and splendour of materials finds ample

[1] *Interpretations of Poetry and Religion*, pp. 176-77.

satisfaction in Swinburne's rhetoric. *Hertha* is indeed a splendid poem and stimulates one side of our nature better than most poems of its kind. But we must not let this splendour blind us to what this kind is.

II

Between *Hertha* and the *Ancient Mariner* there are fewer years than between any other pair of the five poems. Further, we usually think of the Victorian poets as akin to the Romantic. Yet the differences between Coleridge and Swinburne are very great; and, since they illustrate the diversity of currents in the nineteenth century, I will mention some of them.

First, the matter of religion. Even if Coleridge gave hints of pantheism, though he experimented with unitarianism, he wrote his poem in the idiom of orthodoxy, and it is actually grounded on the doctrine of Christian humility. Swinburne is well acquainted with orthodoxy. Had he not been, and had he not known the Bible thoroughly, he could never have rebelled so pointedly. But he certainly does rebel: through his extreme pantheism against orthodox theology, and through his arrogant humanism against Christian ethics. Secondly, although Coleridge had felt the impact of the French Revolution he kept politics out of his best poetry, the *Ancient Mariner* included. Swinburne is very political in *Songs before Sunrise*, expressing the full force of continental revolutionary feeling. And thirdly, Coleridge spoke for his age in minding about the individual and his relation, not so much to society as to his entire setting. Swinburne would certainly have claimed to have inherited the belief in liberal individualism, witness his devotion to Mazzini, but in actual fact he thinks not in terms of the individual but of mankind in the mass.

Some of the differences are simply those between the two poets' characters. But a big balance of them helps to tell us how much had been happening in the seventy years between the two poems. The advance of science, especially the biological and geological, had shaken the old orthodoxies and made possible the jubilation with which Swinburne is able to utter his doctrines of liberty and humanity. The industrial revolution, not fully operant on men's thoughts in 1798, had now really made itself felt and by presenting mankind in great, organised groups had set up a sudden and powerful counter-movement against the still current doctrines of Romantic individualism. These two great happenings, added to the normal human impulse to change, are quite enough to make any differences between Coleridge and Swinburne no matter for surprise. I go on now to some of the matters in which Swinburne represents at least a part of his age.

(a)

SELF-SUFFICIENCY

I have already included *Hertha* in what Santayana calls the Poetry of Barbarism. To bring the position more into the light let me recall the ideas of civility that governed the *Ode on Anne Killigrew*. If *Hertha* is barbarous to Santayana, on how many added grounds would it be so to Dryden. Behind the *Ode* are various fixed assumptions. If you write poetry you select from a fixed repertory of accepted forms. The subject dictates a relatively small number of options among these forms. Anne Killigrew was aristocratic: nothing but a high or at least a dignified form would suit. The formal ode was one of the appropriate forms. To such an ode a certain type of language belonged. When it came to subject-matter a strict decorum ruled. Dryden's poem was written as a preface to Anne Killigrew's poems; hence the obligation to be laudatory. Decorum prescribed a degree of laudation that had nothing to do with the poetic merit of the lady's verses. There was a similar obligation to be extravagant in claiming for her the certainty of heavenly bliss. We are apt to mark such procedure not by the friendly word *decorous* but by the hostile word *mechanical*; and to add that Coleridge substituted a rule of inner propriety and coherence for the old Augustan rule of preconceived outward decorum, turning the *mechanical* into the *organic*. Now the *Ancient Mariner* succeeds so well as a poem that the matter of decorum does not seem to arise. It is in itself so much as it ought to be that any external principles simply cannot make themselves felt: there is no chink in the armour. And Dryden himself, though hopelessly puzzled by the poem could he have read it, might well have refrained from obloquy. Swinburne wrote *Hertha* on the new rule of the inner propriety. He is not tied to a poetic diction: his metre corresponds to his own emotional requirements and not to a dictated precedent. Dryden would have disapproved but might have allowed some credit to the result. But liberty does not stop there. Even if Swinburne has many debts of material—to the East, to Teutonic legend, to the Bible—he owns no poetical master. The only law governing the way he writes and the amount he writes are his own emotions and his arbitrary will. He thus puts an immense weight on his own powers; and even in the act of admiring a prodigious performance, we experience a feeling of strain because we are nervous lest the performer should exceed his powers. It is this arrogant self-sufficiency that Dryden would have found indecorous in the highest degree. I am not suggesting that Swinburne represents all Victorian verse but with Browning and Meredith often open to the same criticism, he does represent some of the most energetic.

(*b*)

PROGRESS

The world in which Henryson lived thought that man's object was to approximate himself to a predetermined scale of perfection. He made a poor show, but the scale by its fixity gave him a sense of stability. For Swinburne, man's object is to keep moving. The nature of things is evolutionary, and man must conform to the evolutionary movement, to the life-force. It is a pleasant doctrine if the evolutionary movement appears to be in a good direction; and Swinburne is gloriously certain that the movement away from creeds and towards liberty of thought was both actual and good. Recently people have not been so certain that things are evolving the right way; and the religion of progress is thus less popular than it was. But it was for a time truly a religion, and Swinburne was of his age in so making it.

It is easy to-day, and it may soon become cheaply fashionable, to jeer at Victorian ideas of progress. But such jeers would apply less to Swinburne than to many, because his beliefs were not those of the complacent acceptors of the doctrine. Indeed his affinities were more with the Continent than with England. Just because Victorian England was so rich and so strong, because so many obvious reforms had been effected, and because she was the world's political leader, her picture of progress was largely material. As she was growing richer more comfortable and more pacific, so other countries would imitate her and do the same. Parliamentary democracy and free trade were so obviously good that they were bound to spread; and men could look forward, without worry, to an ever-increasing measure of prosperity.

Swinburne did not share such complacency, nor could he welcome the visions of a static golden age with its classless society that mitigated the severities of the Marxist creed. He believed that evolution would do away with certain restraints, but not necessarily tend towards greater comfort. Freedom was evolution's inevitable course and hence it was good. Hertha says

> *My growth have no guerdon*
> *But only to grow.*

Not happiness, not comfort, not a refrigerator and a

garage in every home, is the object of life but the removal
of artificial sacerdotal restrictions and the consequent full
surrender to the life-force. Swinburne, in effect, rejects the
Anglo-Saxon version of the religion of progress (still
powerful in the United States of America) and allies himself with a form of it which has had surprising results in
recent years and which has little kinship to the ideas of
liberty which Swinburne felt so strongly about. Swinburne
exhorts man to fulfil the evolutionary process, or his
destiny, and he thought the way was through abolishing
certain restraints. Relying on a different method Mussolini
and Hitler preached the same doctrine of fulfilment. Like
Swinburne, Mussolini affected to spurn the comfortable
things of life—these could be left to the decadent demo-
cracies: what mattered was that Italy should fulfil her
destiny; should embrace that portion of the evolutionary
process that was her share. Hitler considered that the
struggle with Bolshevism, the struggle that was to settle
the shape of the world for a thousand years, was the next
great evolutionary event. After the crisis, which was to
have been the defeat of Bolshevism, perhaps after a hundred, perhaps two hundred, years, man would burst out
into a glory such as had not yet been seen.

Swinburne would never himself have been a Fascist,
but he was the unsuspecting mouthpiece of the ideas out
of which Fascist doctrine was made; just as his unbridled
juvenility represents a state of mind favourable to the
spread of that doctrine. In extenuation of Swinburne
we must remember the immense apparent stability of
Victorian England, a stability that easily could tempt a
revolutionary to be irresponsible.

(c)

TEUTONISM

When Swinburne put the notion of man's coming splendour in terms of blossoms bursting out over Yggdrasil,

the Life-tree, he did something that would have appealed to Hitler and Rosenberg. But he does not merely anticipate: he represents a contemporary movement to exalt the Teutonic over the Latin. German anti-Gallicism was of much earlier origin, but it was about the time of *Songs before Sunrise* that the impulse to purge the German language of romance words grew strong, while the exaltation of Teutonic legend through Wagnerian opera was contemporary with Swinburne's best poetic output. In England the movement was much feebler, consisting of the attempt to exalt *Beowulf* into an English *Iliad* and to strengthen the Anglo-Saxon as against the Latin element in the English vocabulary. People who write *forewords* instead of *prefaces* are the unconscious heirs of the movement.

(d)

THE PAST

It would have been possible, but it would not have been fair, to deduce from the *Ancient Mariner* that enlarged understanding of the past that was one of the genuine marks of the nineteenth century. Coleridge uses an antique setting, which, however remotely, reflects the antiquarian interest in the past that gathered force throughout the eighteenth century, but he does not use both knowledge and imagination in order to see the past as it was and not as the present would like it to be. Swinburne's notion of the past deserves a mention, not because it represents the new enlarged understanding but because it illustrates very well the errors into which advocates of progress are apt to fall when they consider their antecedents. The errors are those of anthologising, of heeding some portions and cutting out the rest. In stanzas thirty and thirty-one we can be sure, from what we know of Swinburne generally, that he refers to the Greeks of the fifth century, that he is anthologising from history the epoch he prefers and does not wish to forget.

HERTHA

In the spring-coloured hours
When my mind was as May's,
There brake forth of me flowers
By centuries of days,
Strong blossoms with perfume of manhood, shot out from
my spirit as rays.

But in stanzas twenty-one and -three he looks on the past
as dead and done with; annihilated and irrelevant:

But the Gods of your fashion
That take and that give,
In their pity and passion
That scourge and forgive,
They are worms that are bred in the bark that falls off; they
shall die and not live.

Where dead ages hide under
The live roots of the tree . . .

In view of the many horrors of history, such a piece of
wishful thinking is natural enough. Let them be wiped
out, and the happier future alone contemplated. Thus
argued many tender-hearted people. But Swinburne was
not one of these, and *his* particular form of wishful thinking was that of a politician in a hurry: the man who cannot
allow the relevance of the past because it upsets his preconceived desire for rapid change. And this is one more
example of the barbarism of Swinburne's poetry. In the
abstract, the idea that the past is any less real than the
present or the future is repellent, however bewildering the
nature of past existence may be. And by common sense
the hope that man may suddenly abjure his own mental
habits as revealed in history will not bear the least scrutiny.

(*e*)

LIBERTY

The habit of ignoring the past leads to Swinburne's
idea of liberty; for just as past ages are to be abolished

and ignored, so must all apparent restraints on man's mind be abolished, on the assumption that they are negative things and can really be wiped out of existence. I should not wish to suggest that on a balance Englishmen had more freedom in 1470 than in 1870, but at least the older conceptions of liberty had certain advantages over Swinburne's. Just as *all* existence, past present and future, found its place somewhere in the chain of being, so the problem of liberty was not one of removing restraints or of ignoring existing institutions but of allowing to all items of existence the fulfilment of which they were capable. In other words liberty consisted not in destruction but in due adjustment.

Swinburne is also clearer on how to get liberty than on what that liberty is when you have got it. In his anxiety to defeat the restraints of sacerdotalism and to establish liberty, he forgets that external liberty evaporates, if the will of those who might enjoy it has been already neutralised: without the larger liberty of the individual mind the smaller liberty from the dictates of ecclesiastical organisation means nothing. Seeking to abolish the tyranny of man over man he fails to see the danger of the greater tyranny of blind forces over the individual. Nor does he see that the tyranny he attacks was the abuse of a religion whose very principle was that superior and essential liberty of will without which those very attacks are futile.

In all this Swinburne was not typical. On a balance the nineteenth century principle of liberty was one of its great characteristic virtues. Swinburne better illustrates its dangers than its virtues, and in so doing anticipates a later age rather than characterises his own.

(f)

MAN NOT MEN

For Coleridge and Wordsworth individualism and liberty were conceptions that went naturally together. Yet experience shows that this is not necessarily so. Any sudden increase in individual responsibility may mean too great a demand on the weaker natures. There follows a state of panic and a quick casting-round for guidance from without. The faint-hearted are then an easy prey for a man or an organisation offering a specious certainty, a simplified creed, and an apparently quick return. Further, the impulse towards individual liberty was soon yoked with one towards other liberties, national and economic. And these other liberties could be obtained only by mass-effort; and such a mass-effort could not fail to endanger the identity of the individual.

Swinburne, though nominally a fierce individualist, does in *Hertha* express the very principles that make individualism impossible. He pictures mankind in the mass and this mass swept in a necessary (if right) direction by the great tide of events. A man, in *Hertha*, is no longer the possessor of a soul, the value of which evades all earthly standards, but one of a vast number of units, not specifically differentiated, whose value lies in the sum they compose. It is the destiny and direction of this sum which alone counts. I do not suggest that Swinburne consciously reached this conclusion, but *Hertha* does indeed suggest the climate in which such totalitarian ideas can flourish. The intoxication of these ideas is well known. To surrender the individual will and the painful business of making choices to what a leader, guiding the group-mind, dictates may bring with it a wonderful sense of release and happiness. And the intoxicating quality of Swinburne's verse represents such a process only too well.

(g)

TRUTH

At the very end of *Hertha* we read that it is truth that kills God and then occupies his position.

> *For truth only is living,*
> *Truth only is whole,*

FIVE POEMS

And the love of his giving
Man's polestar and pole.

In thus writing, Swinburne spoke for his age, for if Progress was one potent Victorian god, Truth was another. Many people worshipped both with the same fervour; but, on the whole, Progress was the god of the social reformers and Truth of the scientists. Truth in that age had two great qualifications as an object of worship. She was persecuted and she demanded great sacrifices. Bigotry and vested interests had tried to impede scientific advancement; and what science had revealed, for instance the evolution of man instead of his instantaneous creation in full maturity or the ultimate extinction of life on this planet, were truths most painful to many people whose consciences forced their acceptance. The only way to compensate for the sacrifice to Truth of dearly loved falsehoods was to exalt Truth herself, for, if the thing to which sacrifice is made is sufficiently august, no sacrifice will be too painful. Thus Clough, a man very sensitive to the conflicts of his age, wrote:

> *It fortifies my soul to know*
> *That, though I perish, Truth is so:*
> *That, howsoe'er I stray and range,*
> *Whate'er I do, Thou dost not change.*
> *I steadier step when I recall*
> *That, if I slip, Thou dost not fall.*

When this worship of Truth was joined with a real sacrifice there was something noble in it and being widespread it forms one of the great virtues of the Victorian age. But as it became easier it degenerated. The extreme worshippers made themselves ridiculous by proscribing everything outside the realm of verifiable fact and banishing fairy tales from the nursery, and for the unreflective it was a simple creed and saved a lot of trouble. As goddess of most nineteenth century scientists it remained a most important influence. In more recent times, when the facts revealed by science have had dangerous results and ordinary men begin to question the good of unrestricted scientific investigation, Truth has still served as the ultimate justification. All personal responsibility in the discoverer could be shed and transferred to the great abstraction. Many scientists to-day refuse to accept such a transfer of responsibility, but it was interesting that the first of the many letters printed in the *Times* on the atomic bomb (and it came from a President of the Royal Society) ended with an appeal to the goddess. Truth came first: nothing must stand in the way of the advancement of knowledge.

It is likely that future ages will look back on the cult of Truth not only as characteristic of a certain age but as a very curious limitation of the human mind. In the traditional psychology the human mind was divided into the provinces of understanding and will. It was necessary for the understanding to be enlightened in order that the will might make proper choices. The erection of scientific truth, which means the data of the understanding, into an abstraction that relieves the human will of its function in making choices, would, by the standard of the traditional psychology, imply a revolutionary truncation of the human attributes. In the vacuum thus created not truth but superstition might all too easily come to flourish.

(*h*)

ENERGY

In writing of *Hertha*'s affinities with contemporary thought I may have appeared mainly derogatory. Indeed when one takes Swinburne in detail it is hard not to be. It is only fair therefore to end by pointing out that his great quality, his energy, though partly personal, does worthily express the astonishing energy of his age also. To many of his age's activities he would have thought himself hostile, and yet of the undefinable urge that prompted these activities he is a most authentic mouthpiece.

EPILOGUE

THE Victorian age was so varied that the risk of falsifying it by seeing it through the medium of a single writer is very great. *Hertha* can suggest only a limited range of contemporary thought. Let it therefore be remembered that in 1870 Arnold published his first book on religion, *St Paul and Protestantism*, and that in 1872 Samuel Butler published *Erewhon*. Both these writers are free from the bigotry Swinburne attacks and from the fanaticism he unconsciously promotes. And let the names of Arnold and Butler, here mentioned in a tone of approval, guard me from a thought which some readers may have acquired in reading this book: that I have been leading up to a plea for a return to medievalism. It cannot be denied that in the nineteenth century conceptions of the universe were multifarious untidy and ugly, while in the Middle Ages they were uniform neat and beautiful. But a return to such simplicity is unthinkable, even if we can admire it from a distance and use it as an analogy to inspire some new adjustment. The sophistication of Arnold and Butler is a better antidote to Swinburne's poetry of barbarism than anything medieval can possibly be. This is not to suggest that mere sophistication can defeat the powers of barbarism: some positive faith is needed as well. It was from Santayana that I borrowed the term "poetry of barbarism" and from the same book[1] I will quote a passage, which, though written half a century ago, has not gone in the least stale. If my remarks in this book should have led up to the questions Santayana asks in this passage, I shall be well content.

Human life is always essentially the same, and therefore a religion which, like Christianity, seizes the essence of that life, ought to be an eternal religion. But it may forfeit that privilege

[1] *Interpretations of Poetry and Religion*, pp. 116-17.

by entangling itself with a particular account of matters of fact, matters irrelevant to its ideal significance, and further by intrenching itself, by virtue of that entanglement, in an inadequate regimen or a too narrow imaginative development, thus putting its ideal authority in jeopardy by opposing it to other intuitions and practices no less religious than its own.

Can Christianity escape these perils? Can it reform its claims, or can it overwhelm all opposition and take the human heart once more by storm? The future alone can decide. The greatest calamity, however, would be that which seems, alas! not unlikely to befall our immediate posterity, namely, that while Christianity should be discredited no other religion, more disillusioned and not less inspired, should come to take its place. Until the imagination should have time to recover and reassert its legitimate and kindly power, the European races would then be reduced to confessing that while they had mastered the mechanical forces of Nature, both by science and by the arts, they had become incapable of mastering or understanding themselves, and that, bewildered like the beasts by the revolutions of the heavens and by their own irrational passions, they could find no way of uttering the ideal meaning of their life.

NOTES ON THE ILLUSTRATIONS

1. *Parting of Troilus and Cressida*

This comes from an illustration in a manuscript of Lydgate's *Troy Book*. The manuscript is in the British Museum (Royal 18 D ii) and dates about 1450.

The scene is outside one of the gates of Troy. It is the final parting of the lovers. Troilus clasps Cressida's waist, while Cressida presses one hand to her breast and with the other tears her hair. In the centre Troilus's squire, holding his lance, watches the lovers with a mournful expression. Behind him other Trojans watch the scene. On the right stand a man and woman, whom Lydgate's text does not help to identify. Probably the man is Diomede, come to fetch Cressida, and he is making the best use of his time by holding an animated conversation with a Trojan lady.

The illustration is not a great work of art, but it is a clearly composed scene, and the gay colouring recalls the brilliance of some of Henryson's descriptions. Diomede and Troilus's squire remind us of "the royal rinks in thair array, in garmentis gay", while the pleasing glimpse of landscape and the flowery foreground remind us of Cressida's walking out in the early morning "to tak the dew". Cressida's conventional gestures of grief correspond to Troilus's conventional love-signs when the sight of the leprous Cressida arouses in him the relics of his old passion.

But these are secondary resemblances. The fundamental resemblance is the serenity of tone. Lydgate's illustrator accumulates his details—the dresses, the flowers in the foreground, the windows in the walls and battlements, the little tree growing on one of the ruinous towers—with the assurance and the leisure of a man bred in a world whose principles were accepted without question. He does not need to worry, he can go on compiling and elaborating.

NOTES ON ILLUSTRATIONS

2. *Mural Tablet of John Law*

BY NICHOLAS STONE

The tablet is in the chapel of the Charterhouse in London and is dated 1615. It is illustrated in Plate V of the seventh volume of the Walpole Society Publications, which is a study of Nicholas Stone by W. L. Spiers, published 1919.

It is not too easy to find good art-analogies with Davies's *Orchestra*. Elizabethan pictures are too factual and too little fanciful. The exuberance of the funerary monuments give better scope. Here is a monument—rather on the late side but maintaining the Elizabethan tradition—that does convey better than most that Elizabethan mixture of the solid and the fantastic which marked *Orchestra*. Perched high on top, the merry little Cupid astride a skull gives the right suggestion of violent contrast. What surrounds the central effigy is all grace and fancy: the beautifully curved frame with its volutes above and below, the elegant willowy angels with their postures hinting at the dance and their charmingly fussy, negligent drapery. But the central figure is uncompromising in his stolid seriousness, and the heavy and decided folds of his jacket contradict the weak elegance of the flanking figures. It is no mere convention that the lower extremity of the frame should be filled with a skull, which is a true *memento mori* with all its religious connotations.

In sum the solidity of the central figure with its serious and religious asseverations corresponds to the basic seriousness of the world picture in *Orchestra*, while the figure's circumference with the piping Cupid above correspond to the wealth of extravagant fancy that marks the poem.

3. *Chimney-Piece at Belton House*

BY GRINLING GIBBONS

It is illustrated in fig. 190 of H. A. Tipping's book on Grinling Gibbons (London 1914).

Sir John Brownlow began building Belton House (near Grantham) in 1685 with Wren as architect and Grinling Gibbons as wood carver. The chimney-piece would thus be almost exactly contemporary with Dryden's *Ode on Anne Killigrew*. The portrait within the chimney-piece is that of Margaret, Sir John Brownlow's fourth daughter.

There is a strong resemblance between Dryden's *Ode* and the portrait with its setting at Belton, in that in both works it is the setting and the ornamentation that transcend the supposed subject. Just as Anne Killigrew exists less in her own right than as the pretext for poetry, so Margaret Brownlow's portrait exists to give a reason for the much more important work of art that surrounds it.

But there is a more fundamental resemblance and one that typifies a general kinship of spirit between the work of Dryden and of Gibbons. The chimney-piece with its crowded details of still-life, duck snipe pheasant, flowers fruit ears of corn, and the rest, is excessively ornate, in a way outrageous; and yet that ornateness does not at all conflict with the sobriety of the mantelpiece it surmounts, of the picture-frame it surrounds, and of the panelling on which it is superimposed. The wings of the birds go so far as to break into the perpendicular lines of panelling and frame, yet they do not thereby disturb the fundamental good sense of the total scheme. Rather they enhance it, just as a touch of negligence or oddity was thought necessary to complete the excellence of refined manners. Dryden shares this spirit. His extravagances of expression are subordinate to his formal solidity and correct sentiments and in this subordination serve to heighten the very things they may appear to contradict.

Finally, the bold contours of the carving with their strong tactile attraction correspond to the noble resounding quality of Dryden's verse. A splendid and similar energy informs both verse and carving.

4. *The Witches in* Macbeth

BY HENRY FUSELI

This is a pen and brush drawing now in the Kunsthaus at Zurich. It is reproduced on Plate 45 of A. Federmann's *Johann Heinrich Füssli* (Zurich 1927).

Fuseli, whose real name was Füssli, was a native of Zurich. He is the contemporary of Blake rather than of Coleridge, but he did not die till 1825. He lived much of his life in England and about the time the *Ancient Mariner* was published became professor of painting at the Royal Academy. The strength and wildness of his imagination make him typical of the Romantic movement.

The drawing represents the three Witches being swept on a dark cloud across the place where the naked figures of Macbeth and Banquo are standing. A part of the cloud below has taken the shape of a vulture or some bird of prey. Below, on the right, the battle is indicated by a vague confusion of people (one of them mounted and wearing a classical helmet) blowing trumpets. A great hand appears behind them pointing upwards. The Witches point with unnaturally lengthened forefingers at Macbeth, who strains towards them extending his right arm. Banquo draws himself up and back, as if in recoil from the Witches, and holds up a (symbolical?) torch.

There is a good deal in common between the world of Fuseli's drawing and that of the *Ancient Mariner*. A powerful sense of the supernatural pervades both. The Witches are less like old women and nearer to vague terrifying presences than Shakespeare conceived them. They approximate to the supernatural creatures of Coleridge's poem. There is also the sense of fatality. Macbeth, like the Ancient Mariner, is the victim of a doom. But the proud and free figure of Banquo suggests the possibility of freedom and regeneration. Above all Fuseli's drawing creates an exciting and mysterious world, whose limits cannot be precisely drawn, whose nature is marvellous, remote from the confinedly material and pervaded by the vaguely numinous.

5. *Automedon with the Horses of Achilles*

BY HENRI REGNAULT

Regnault was born six years after Swinburne and he was killed in the Franco-Prussian War. He painted this picture (now in the Boston Museum of Fine Arts) in 1868 at Rome. Swinburne began *Songs before Sunrise* at that time and derived part of his inspiration from Italy.

The scene is on the sea-shore with the Trojan foothills rising on the left. Automedon has been having trouble with the horses but he has already got one under control and is well on his way to taming the more formidable black prancer.

The analogy with *Hertha* is so obvious as scarcely to need mention. A sense of drama, of violent and significant happenings, animates (or is intended to animate) both works. The atmosphere of the picture with its black shadows and streaks of light is tense and lurid. The horses are wild and "elemental", filled with the energy of Mother Earth, blossoms on the "tree many-rooted". But the full limelight is reserved for the human figure: glory to Man, the consummation of the evolutionary process.

NOTES ON ILLUSTRATIONS

A passage from one of Regnault's letters written in Rome about Michelangelo confirms this glorification of Man.

Que voulez-vous qu'on fasse quand on se trouve en face de ce géant ? Que peut-on oser devant lui, quand on est écrasé sous un double sentiment d'étonnement et d'admiration tellement étrange qu'on se demande si ce n'est pas de la peur ? Pour moi, Michel-Ange est un dieu auquel on ne doit pas toucher; on craindrait qu'il n'en sortît du feu.

Finally, I spoke in the text of Swinburne's continental affinities. It is therefore apt that the best analogy I could find with *Hertha* came from a French and not an English brush.

Appendix I

JOHN DRYDEN

To the Pious Memory of the Accomplished Young Lady
MRS. ANNE KILLIGREW

I

Thou youngest virgin-daughter of the skies,
Made in the last promotion of the blest;
 Whose palms, new plucked from Paradise,
In spreading branches more sublimely rise,
Rich with immortal green above the rest:
Whether. adopted to some neighbouring star,
Thou roll'st above us in thy wandering race,
Or in procession fixed and regular
 Moved with the heaven's majestic pace,
 Or called to more superior bliss,
Thou tread'st with seraphims the vast abyss:
Whatever happy region be thy place,
Cease thy celestial song a little space;
Thou wilt have time enough for hymns divine,
 Since Heaven's eternal year is thine.
Hear then a mortal Muse thy praise rehearse
  In no ignoble verse,
But such as thy own voice did practise here,
When thy first fruits of poesy were given,
To make thyself a welcome inmate there;
 While yet a young probationer,
  And candidate of Heaven.

2

 If by traduction came thy mind,
 Our wonder is the less to find
A soul so charming from a stock so good;
Thy father was transfused into thy blood:
So wert thou born into the tuneful strain,
(An early, rich, and inexhausted vein.)

But if thy pre-existing soul
Was formed at first with myriads more,
It did through all the mighty poets roll
Who Greek or Latin laurels wore,
And was that Sappho last, which once it was before.
If so, then cease thy flight, O heaven-born mind!
Thou hast no dross to purge from thy rich ore:
Nor can thy soul a fairer mansion find
Than was the beauteous frame she left behind:
Return, to fill or mend the quire of thy celestial kind.

3

May we presume to say that, at thy birth,
New joy was sprung in heaven as well as here on earth?
For sure the milder planets did combine
On thy auspicious horoscope to shine,
And even the most malicious were in trine.
Thy brother-angels at thy birth
Strung each his lyre, and tuned it high,
That all the people of the sky
Might know a poetess was born on earth;
And then, if ever, mortal ears
Had heard the music of the spheres.
And if no clustering swarm of bees
On thy sweet mouth distilled their golden dew,
'Twas that such vulgar miracles
Heaven had not leisure to renew:
For all the blest fraternity of love
Solemnized there thy birth, and kept thy holiday above.

4

O gracious God! how far have we
Profaned thy heavenly gift of Poesy!
Made prostitute and profligate the Muse,
Debased to each obscene and impious use,
Whose harmony was first ordained above,
For tongues of angels and for hymns of love!
Oh wretched we! why were we hurried down
This lubric and adulterate age,
(Nay, added fat pollutions of our own,)
To increase the steaming ordures of the stage?

FIVE POEMS

What can we say to excuse our second fall?
Let this thy Vestal, Heaven, atone for all:
Her Arethusian stream remains unsoiled,
Unmixed with foreign filth and undefiled;
Her wit was more than man, her innocence a child.

5

Art she had none, yet wanted none,
For Nature did that want supply:
So rich in treasures of her own,
She might our boasted stores defy:
Such noble vigour did her verse adorn
That it seemed borrowed, where 'twas only born.
Her morals too were in her bosom bred,
By great examples daily fed,
What in the best of books, her father's life, she read.
And to be read herself she need not fear;
Each test and every light her Muse will bear,
Though Epictetus with his lamp were there.
Even love (for love sometimes her Muse exprest)
Was but a lambent flame which played about her breast:
Light as the vapours of a morning dream,
So cold herself, whilst she such warmth exprest,
'Twas Cupid bathing in Diana's stream.

6

Born to the spacious empire of the Nine,
One would have thought she should have been content
To manage well that mighty government;
But what can young ambitious souls confine?
To the next realm she stretched her sway,
For Painture near adjoining lay,
A plenteous province and alluring prey.
A Chamber of Dependences was framed,
(As conquerors will never want pretence,
When armed, to justify the offence),
And the whole fief in right of Poetry she claimed.
The country open lay without defence;
For poets frequent inroads there had made,
And perfectly could represent
The shape, the face, with every lineament,

And all the large domains which the dumb sister swayed;
    All bowed beneath her government,
   Received in triumph wheresoe'er she went.
   Her pencil drew whate'er her soul designed,
And oft the happy draught surpassed the image in her mind.
      The sylvan scenes of herds and flocks
      And fruitful plains and barren rocks;
      Of shallow brooks that flowed so clear,
      The bottom did the top appear;
      Of deeper too and ampler floods
      Which, as in mirrors, showed the woods;
      Of lofty trees, with sacred shades
      And perspectives of pleasant glades,
      Where nymphs of brightest form appear,
      And shaggy satyrs standing near,
      Which them at once admire and fear.
   The ruins too of some majestic piece,
   Boasting the power of ancient Rome or Greece,
   Whose statues, friezes, columns, broken lie,
   And, though defaced, the wonder of the eye;
   What nature, art, bold fiction, e'er durst frame,
   Her forming hand gave feature to the name.
   So strange a concourse ne'er was seen before,
But when the peopled ark the whole creation bore.

7

   The scene then changed; with bold erected look
   Our martial King the sight with reference strook:
   For, not content to express his outward part,
   Her hand called out the image of his heart:
   His warlike mind, his soul devoid of fear,
   His high-designing thoughts were figured there,
   As when by magic ghosts are made appear.
   Our phoenix queen was portrayed too so bright,
   Beauty alone could beauty take so right:
      Her dress, her shape, her matchless grace,
   Were all observed, as well as heavenly face.
   With such a peerless majesty she stands,
As in that day she took the crown from sacred hands;
   Before a train of heroines, was seen
   In beauty foremost, as in rank, the queen.

Thus nothing to her genius was denied,
But like a ball of fire, the farther thrown,
   Still with a greater blaze she shone,
And her bright soul broke out on every side.
What next she had designed, Heaven only knows:
To such immoderate growth her conquest rose
That Fate alone its progress could oppose.

8

   Now all those charms, that blooming grace,
The well-proportioned shape and beauteous face,
Shall never more be seen by mortal eyes;
In earth the much-lamented virgin lies.
Not wit nor piety could Fate prevent;
Nor was the cruel Destiny content
To finish all the murder at a blow,
To sweep at once her life and beauty too;
But, like a hardened felon, took a pride
   To work more mischievously slow,
   And plundered first, and then destroyed,
O double sacrilege on things divine,
To rob the relic, and deface the shrine!
   But thus Orinda died:
Heaven by the same disease did both translate;
As equal were their souls, so equal was their fate.

9

Meantime, her warlike brother on the seas
His waving streamers to the winds displays,
And vows for his return with vain devotion pays.
   Ah, generous youth! that wish forbear,
   The winds too soon will waft thee here!
   Slack all thy sails, and fear to come;
Alas! thou knowst not, thou art wrecked at home.
No more shalt thou behold thy sister's face,
Thou hast already had her last embrace.
But look aloft, and if thou kenst from far,
Among the Pleiads, a new-kindled star,
If any sparkles than the rest more bright,
'Tis she that shines in that propitious light.

10

When in mid-air the golden trump shall sound,
   To raise the nations under ground;
When in the Valley of Jehosophat
The judging God shall close the book of Fate,
   And there the last assizes keep
   For those who wake and those who sleep;
   When rattling bones together fly
   From the four corners of the sky;
When sinews o'er the skeletons are spread,
Those clothed with flesh, and life inspires the dead;
The sacred poets first shall hear the sound,
   And foremost from the tomb shall bound,
For they are covered with the lightest ground;
And straight, with inborn vigour, on the wing,
Like mounting larks, to the new morning sing.
There thou, sweet saint, before the quire shalt go,
As harbinger of Heaven, the way to show,
The way which thou so well hast learned below.

Appendix II

A. C. SWINBURNE

Hertha

1

I am that which began;
　　Out of me the years roll;
Out of me God and man;
　　I am equal and whole;
God changes, and man, and the form of them bodily;
　　I am the soul.

2

Before ever land was,
　　Before ever the sea,
Or soft hair of the grass,
　　Or fair limbs of the tree,
Or the flesh-coloured fruit of my branches, I was,
　　and thy soul was in me.

3

First life on my sources
　　First drifted and swam;
Out of me are the forces
　　That save it or damn;
Out of me man and woman, and wild-beast and
　　bird: before God was, I am.

4

Beside or above me
　　Nought is there to go;
Love or unlove me,
　　Unknow me or know,
I am that which unloves me and loves; I am
　　stricken, and I am the blow.

APPENDIX II

5

I the mark that is missed
    And the arrows that miss,
I the mouth that is kissed
    And the breath in the kiss,
The search, and the sought, and the seeker, the
    soul and the body that is.

6

I am that thing which blesses
    My spirit elate;
That which caresses
    With hands uncreate
My limbs unbegotten that measure the length of
    the measure of fate.

7

But what thing dost thou now,
    Looking Godward, to cry
"I am I, thou art thou,
    I am low, thou art high"?
I am thou, whom thou seekest to find him; find
    thou but thyself, thou art I.

8

I the grain and the furrow,
    The plough-cloven clod
And the ploughshare drawn thorough,
    The germ and the sod,
The deed and the doer, the seed and the sower,
    the dust which is God.

9

Hast thou known how I fashioned thee,
    Child, underground?
Fire that impassioned thee,
    Iron that bound,
Dim changes of water, what thing of all these hast
    thou known of or found?

10

Canst thou say in thine heart
  Thou hast seen with thine eyes
With what cunning of art
  Thou wast wrought in what wise,
By what force of what stuff thou wast shapen,
  and shown on my breast to the skies?

11

Who hath given, who hath sold it thee,
  Knowledge of me?
Has the wilderness told it thee?
  Hast thou learnt of the sea?
Hast thou communed in spirit with night? have
  the winds taken counsel with thee?

12

Have I set such a star
  To show light on thy brow
That thou sawest from afar
  What I show to thee now?
Have ye spoken as brethren together, the sun and
  the mountains and thou?

13

What is here, dost thou know it?
  What was, hast thou known?
Prophet nor poet
  Nor tripod nor throne
Nor spirit nor flesh can make answer, but only thy
  mother alone.

14

Mother, not maker,
  Born, and not made;
Though her children forsake her,
  Allured or afraid,
Praying prayers to the God of their fashion, she
  stirs not for all that have prayed.

15

A creed is a rod,
    And a crown is of night;
But this thing is God,
    To be man with thy might,
To grow straight in the strength of thy spirit, and
    live out thy life as the light.

16

I am in thee to save thee,
    As my soul in thee saith;
Give thou as I gave thee,
    Thy life-blood and breath,
Green leaves of thy labour, white flowers of thy
    thought, and red fruit of thy death.

17

Be the ways of thy giving
    As mine were to thee;
The free life of thy living,
    Be the gift of it free;
Not as servant to lord, nor as master to slave,
    shalt thou give thee to me.

18

O children of banishment,
    Souls overcast,
Were the lights ye see vanish meant
    Alway to last,
Ye would know not the sun overshining the
    shadows and stars overpast.

19

I that saw where ye trod
    The dim paths of the night
Set the shadow called God
    In your skies to give light;
But the morning of manhood is risen, and the
    shadowless soul is in sight.

FIVE POEMS

20

The tree many-rooted
That swells to the sky
With frondage red-fruited,
The life-tree am I;
In the buds of your lives is the sap of my leaves:
ye shall live and not die.

21

But the Gods of your fashion
That take and that give,
In their pity and passion
That scourge and forgive,
They are worms that are bred in the bark that falls
off; they shall die and not live.

22

My own blood is what stanches
The wounds in my bark;
Stars caught in my branches
Make day of the dark,
And are worshipped as suns till the sunrise shall
tread out their fires as a spark.

23

Where dead ages hide under
The live roots of the tree,
In my darkness the thunder
Makes utterance of me;
In the clash of my boughs with each other ye hear
the waves sound of the sea.

24

That noise is of Time,
As his feathers are spread
And his feet set to climb
Through the boughs overhead,
And my foliage rings round him and rustles, and
branches are bent with his tread.

25

The storm-winds of ages
  Blow through me and cease,
The war-wind that rages,
  The spring-wind of peace,
Ere the breath of them roughen my tresses, ere one
  of my blossoms increase.

26

All sounds of all changes,
  All shadows and lights
On the world's mountain-ranges
  And stream-riven heights,
Whose tongue is the wind's tongue and language
  of storm-clouds on earth-shaking nights;

27

All forms of all faces,
  All works of all hands
In unsearchable places
  Of time-stricken lands,
All death and all life, and all reigns and all ruins,
  drop through me as sands.

28

Though sore be my burden
  And more than ye know,
And my growth have no guerdon
  But only to grow,
Yet I fail not of growing for lightnings above me
  or deathworms below.

29

These too have their part in me,
  As I too in these;
Such fire is at heart in me,
  Such sap is this tree's,
Which hath in it all sounds and all secrets of infinite
  lands and of seas.

30

In the spring-coloured hours
When my mind was as May's,
There brake forth of me flowers
By centuries of days,
Strong blossoms with perfume of manhood, shot
out from my spirit as rays.

31

And the sound of them springing
And smell of their shoots
Were as warmth and sweet singing
And strength to my roots;
And the lives of my children made perfect with
freedom of soul were my fruits.

32

I bid you but be;
I have need not of prayer;
I have need of you free
As your mouths of mine air;
That my heart may be greater within me, behold-
ing the fruits of me fair.

33

More fair than strange fruit is
Of faiths ye espouse;
In me only the root is
That blooms in your boughs;
Behold now your God that ye made you, to feed
him with faith of your vows.

34

In the darkening and whitening
Abysses adored,
With dayspring and lightning
For lamp and for sword,
God thunders in heaven, and his angels are red with
the wrath of the Lord.

35

O my sons, O too dutiful
　　Towards Gods not of me,
Was not I enough beautiful?
　　Was it hard to be free?
For behold, I am with you, am in you and of you;
　　look forth now and see.

36

Lo, winged with world's wonders,
　　With miracles shod,
With the fires of his thunders
　　For raiment and rod,
God trembles in heaven, and his angels are white
　　with the terror of God.

37

For his twilight is come on him,
　　His anguish is here;
And his spirits gaze dumb on him,
　　Grown grey from his fear;
And his hour taketh hold on him stricken, the
　　last of his infinite year.

38

Thought made him and breaks him,
　　Truth slays and forgives;
But to you, as time takes him,
　　This new thing it gives,
Even love, the beloved Republic, that feeds upon
　　freedom and lives.

39

For truth only is living,
　　Truth only is whole,
And the love of his giving
　　Man's polestar and pole;
Man, pulse of my centre, and fruit of my body,
　　and seed of my soul.

40

One birth of my bosom;
One beam of mine eye;
One topmost blossom
That scales the sky;
Man, equal and one with me, man that is made of
me, man that is I.

INDEX

127

FIVE POEMS